How Balcony Gardening Saved My Marriage

A Guide to Gardening at Any Age

Robert K. Branton

HOW BALCONY GARDENING SAVED MY MARRIAGE

Copyright © 2022 by Robert K. Branton.

All rights reserved. Printed in the United States of America. No part of this book may be used or reproduced in any manner whatsoever without written permission except in the case of brief quotations embodied in critical articles or reviews.

CONTENTS

INTRODUCTION 1

CHAPTER ONE 3

GETTING STARTED 3

CHAPTER TWO 32

HOW TO CREATE AND PLANT YOUR CONTAINERS 32

CHAPTER THREE 72

MAINTENANCE OF YOUR CONTAINERS 72

CHAPTER FOUR 96

TROUBLESHOOTING 96

CHAPTER FIVE 130

SEASONAL AND HARVESTING CONSIDERATIONS 130

CHAPTER SIX 136

ADDITIONAL CONTAINER CONCEPTS 136

HOW BALCONY GARDENING SAVED MY MARRIAGE

INTRODUCTION

No marriage is free of issues, that much is certain. Every relationship has its ups and downs. And unlike what Hollywood tries to convince you of, nobody in the real world has constant feelings of fulfillment or love. However, those who have survived "the stress and heat of the day" and gone on to avoid a divorce share three characteristics time and time again.

A resolve to prevent divorce that is spiritually based and endures despite conflicts, suffering, and denial as well as changes and pressures.

When there is genuine, intimate sharing between two people, however infrequent, it seems worth the struggle. (This could refer to one's sense of spiritual well-being despite the partner's seeming lack of appreciation or responsiveness.)

HOW BALCONY GARDENING SAVED MY MARRIAGE

You must be willing to invest the time and effort necessary to save your marriage. Radical changes and patience are frequently required for this.

I will tell you how balcony gardening saved my marriage from crashing in this book. My wife loves the balcony garden, but I never loved it, resulting in many arguments and fights between us because she wanted it on our balcony, which I never wanted.

I thought my wife never loved me until my friend recommended a therapist, who told me what to do that saved my marriage and brought back peace and love back into our home. I learned balcony gardening without my wife's consent ad started the garden in our home which brought butterflies to my wife.

Today, I and my wife are a great team working tirelessly to make our garden a heaven on earth.

Seat back and enjoy all the balcony gardening tips that saved my marriage and you can go ahead and do yours and make your balcony and home a heaven on earth.

CHAPTER ONE

Getting Started

The fact that everyone can cultivate in containers is its best feature. You don't require much room, either time or money to grow a couple of planters full of lovely plants. The only things you need are a desire to grow anything, some inspiration, a little ingenuity, and a few dollars (and Hell, if you're ready to be creative, you can even check that last one off the list). This book has all the knowledge you require to successfully cultivate a variety of plants, including flowers, fruits, vegetables, herbs, and more. Without needing a garden area, container gardening is an excellent entry point for beginners into the world of gardening. Alternatively, for more seasoned gardeners, it's a great method to upgrade your current outdoor living area without spending much time or money. The benefits of preparing your container garden before you begin will go far beyond just producing some attractive plants.

By carefully choosing what to grow and how to grow it, you'll be able to harvest your own fresh, homegrown produce month after month or take pleasure in the year-round color of ornamental flower- and foliage-filled containers while offering habitat for butterflies, bees, hummingbirds, and many other living creatures. Growing in containers has numerous advantages, but to make use of them, you must start with the fundamentals, which take us to the subject of this chapter: getting started.

THE THREE ELEMENTS OF EFFECTIVE CONTAINER GARDENING

Planning is key whether you're growing tropical flowers, evergreen shrubs, or edible plants in your container garden. Putting some thought into creating a solid foundation for your plants is the first step in producing a successful container garden. Poor planning and ignorance of the significance of giving your plants the best possible start can lead to many unsuccessful container gardens. Gardeners sometimes overlook the crucial things that must be in place before even considering planting a single seed because we get so excited about the actual planting procedure. We enjoy strolling through the garden center and choosing the most beautiful plants We frequently neglect choosing the proper potting soil, for example, instead poring over seed catalogs in search of the ideal pepper type. It's a lot of fun to choose plants, place seeds in pots, and bury roots in the dirt, but it's not as much fun to take care of the minute details. However, all those lovely plants and ideal seeds will be unhappy if you ignore the less glamorous activities that are the subject of this chapter, and you will become a gardener who is dissatisfied and frustrated.

The cornerstone of effective container gardening is made up of three pillars, and without them, your chances of having a fruitful container garden are significantly diminished. Things might not go according to plan if you don't use the appropriate container, potting soil, and location. The remaining portions of this chapter thoroughly examine each of these three pillars and provide you with the knowledge required to build a solid foundation for your container garden.

Selection of a Container

There are well over five million results for "container gardening" in a quick internet search. A lot of them start by saying that you can use pretty much anything that can store soil as a garden container. This isn't always the best counsel even though it might be the case.

It might deceive a novice gardener into believing that she can successfully grow almost any kind of plant in almost any container, but this is untrue. Yes, you may use a tea kettle, a boot, or a coffee cup as a container, but will your plants thrive in such a little container?

Naturally, the answer is "maybe." A little container, like a boot or a coffee mug, can do just fine if you're planting a tiny, drought-resistant succulent plant. A tea kettle, however, is a horrible idea if you're trying to grow a watermelon vine. Instead of pushing people to pick the cutest or cleverest item as a container, the emphasis should be on choosing the ideal container for the task at hand.

The next project demonstrates that you can still use inventive materials as containers; all you need to do is choose the correct plants to grow in them. Making wise choices about what to grow in this gutter garden will ensure that it is a successful undertaking. Gutter gardens are excellent vertical container plantings.

GUTTER GARDEN

This project will be very useful to gardeners who have restricted areas. A gutter garden can be grown anywhere there is a wall or a fence.

This idea can be modified in a variety of ways, such as by altering the gutters' length, including more layers of gutters, arranging them in a pattern, or even painting them.

The most crucial thing to remember is choosing the proper plants to fill it. Look for plants that only reach a few inches in height and can tolerate having their roots in confined spaces because the amount of dirt in the gutter is so minimal. You shouldn't cultivate large plants in a gutter garden. Choose a variety of miniature flowers, foliage plants, and foods instead. The following plants were utilized for this project:

'Spicy Globe' Ocimum basilicum, a type of dwarf basil
- Thyme (Thymus vulgaris)
- Delicate marjoram (Origanum majorana)

Salvia officinalis 'Tricolor', often known as Tri-Color Sage
- Lysimachia nummularia 'Aurea', also known as the Golden Creeping Jenny
- Portola (Portulaca grandiflora)
- Curly Juncus, also known as Juncus effusus 'Spiralis'
- Small ivy (Hedera helix cultivar)

Miniature Swiss chard

Because the gutters will be heavy once filled with moist dirt and growing plants, make sure the fence or wall where you wish to put your gutter garden is strong and safe. To achieve the tightest fit, only use mounting brackets made for the gutter type you buy.

There's no need to remove your gutter garden at the end of the season.

The gutters themselves are resistant to the elements. Simply remove any plants with frost damage and throw away the used potting soil. Replant with a new batch of plants when the next spring arrives after refilling with fresh potting soil.

MAKE A Gutter Garden: Instructions

STEP 1 Place the gutter sections on a soft surface and pierce multiple drainage holes in the bottom of each gutter with a hammer and scratch awl.

STEP 2 Carefully align the gutter end caps as you push them over the exposed ends of both gutter sections so that they glide into position.

STEP 3 To keep the gutter end caps in place, run a bead of silicon caulking around the inside seam. Before mounting and installing the gutters, allow the caulking to dry.

STEP 4: Using a level, position one gutter piece against the mounting surface so that its flat side faces the rear. Verify the gutter's level. Mark the gutter's complete top edge on the mounting surface with a marker or pencil. Put the gutter aside after marking the line.

STEP 5 Measure and mark the locations for the mounting brackets using a tape measure. Place the outer brackets about 5 inches from the ends of the gutter, then mark two additional brackets for the 6-foot length of the gutter, one middle bracket for the 4-foot gutter, and two additional brackets evenly spaced apart.

STEP 6: Attach the gutter mounting brackets with screws. Place the brackets slightly lower than the specified line so that the upper edge of the gutter will lie slightly above the top edge of the brackets. Depending on the kind of gutters you have, the distance will change. (Notice: For modified bracket-mounting instructions if you're mounting your gutter garden on a brick or concrete wall, see the note on page 20.)

STEP 7: Mount the gutters into them once all the brackets have been installed. Ensure that the gutters are dangling equal distances on either side of the end mounting brackets, or around 5 inches. Depending on the gutter type, there may be a difference in the attachment technique. Some fit into the mounting brackets by snapping down, while others might require screws, and still, others might just lay there loosely. Half of the gutters should be filled with the 50/50 mixture of compost and potting soil.

STEP 8 Remove the plants from their containers and place them carefully in the gutters, making sure you are satisfied with the arrangement. Once the gutters are almost full, add more potting soil mixture to fill in the spaces between the plants. To prevent irrigation water from dripping off the edge of the gutter, make sure to leave a small gap there.

STEP 9. Water the plants thoroughly. If you planted edible greens or herbs in your gutter garden, make sure to harvest them frequently to prevent them from getting too big for the gutters. Throughout the growing season, keep your gutter garden well-watered because the soil there will dry out more frequently than in larger containers due to its limited volume.

NOTE: The bracket will need to be adjusted if you're placing your gutter garden on a brick or concrete wall.

mounting components: Use 2-inch screws with masonry anchors in place of wood screws. Use a drill with a masonry bit to create a pilot hole for the screw anchors at each of the designated places. The bit you select should match the size of the screw anchor you're using (this is often noted on the package they come in).

After that, place a masonry anchor in each of the previously made pilot holes. Till the lip is flush with the wall, lightly tap it with a hammer. With the holes lined up, set a bracket over each of the masonry anchors, and then use a drill bit to drive the bracket into place.

When choosing the kind of pots to utilize for your container garden, there are several factors to consider. Although physical beauty undoubtedly plays a significant role in the choice, there are other, more crucial considerations.

Let's talk about each of them individually.

Size

To emphasize the significance of size when it comes to container gardening, I'll avoid the apparent cliche and instead list the reasons why it matters so much. First off, larger pots accommodate more potting mix, and the more potting mix a given container can accommodate, the more root growth that container can sustain. A containerized plant is happy and healthy if its roots are deep enough to get nutrients and water and are wide enough to cover the entire container. Because they are healthier overall and less susceptible to stress, plants with deep root systems are less attractive to pests and are better able to fend off diseases.

The term "pot-bound" refers to plants whose roots are tightly packed and looping around the inside of the pot. These plants are more vulnerable to the negative effects of root competition, drought, and nutritional shortages. To put it another way, potted plants experience a lot of stress. Like people, stressed plants have weakened immune systems, making them more vulnerable to pathogens and pests that eat plants. No matter what you're planting, the simplest method to promote strong, fruitful plants is to select a container that can accommodate a year's worth of root growth. Because their weak root systems are unable to support any additional top growth, plants planted in small pots sometimes "max out" at a given height rather than developing to their full potential. Most of the time When plants are forced into tiny containers, vegetable yields are dramatically decreased. Without a doubt, plants grown in containers and in soil that is adequate to sustain their root systems function optimally.

The requirement for water is significantly decreased by using bigger containers. Larger pots may absorb and hold more water because they can accommodate more potting soil. This is particularly true if you use a premium potting mix, such as those that are covered later in this chapter. All of this may be expressed as a simple equation: larger containers = more soil = less watering. Of course, other elements play a role in this equation as well, such as how "thirsty" a specific plant is, how much sun the pot gets, whether the pot is built of a porous material, and whether the pot is exposed to drying winds. However, in general, larger pots require less frequent stirring.

This general rule of thumb is crucial to keep in mind when selecting a container, but I'll go over all the specifics on watering your container plant in Chapter 3.

Of course, the mature size of the plant itself is directly related to the ideal size for a container. A container that holds one or two liters of potting soil is more than enough space for the roots of a tiny lettuce plant (Lactuca sativa), for instance. But if you're cultivating a fig or a huge tropical hibiscus (Hibiscus rosa-Sinensis). It may take some trial and error to determine the best container size for a given plant (or group of plants), but it's always preferable to have a larger pot than one that is too small.

When choosing plants for your container, I suggest referring to the instructions for each type of plant on the following page. The container sizes listed here hold the bare minimum amount of soil that each plant in question requires. These measurements must be added together if multiple plants will be in the same pot so that there is enough room for each plant to develop a healthy root system. A container that holds at least 20 to 28 gallons of the potting mix is required if you wish to grow a tomato plant (Solanum Lycopersicum), a pepper plant (Capsicum spp.), and a few herbs together. These are recommendations, not rules since the specific variety of any given vegetable also has a significant impact on the size container it requires. For example, while it's obvious that a determinate or dwarf tomato will require a much larger pot than a standard-sized tomato does, it's still best to err on the side of caution.

The next chapter goes deeper into the topic of pot size by introducing you to certain fruit and vegetable kinds that were specifically engineered to be grown in containers. This is done because of the substantial variation among species of plants. These options are ideal for container gardeners who wish to conserve space by using smaller pots or by growing more plants in each container because they are smaller in stature and have more compact growth. You have all the information you need to decide which plants would be the greatest fit for every given pot if you combine the data below with the varietal data in the following chapter.

Minimum Required Soil Volume for Particular Plants:
• A minimum of 30 gallons per evergreen, tiny shade tree, or dwarf fruit tree.

• A minimum of 20 to 30 gallons per shrub or another large plant, such as figs, blueberries (Vaccinium spp.), goji berries (Lycium spp.), hydrangeas (Hydrangea spp.), tropical blooming plants, and many others.

• 10 to 15 gallons are required at the very least for each extra-large vegetable, such as full-sized tomatoes, winter squash (Cucurbita spp.), pumpkins (Cucurbita spp.), melons (Cucumis melo), and artichokes.
• 8 to 10 gallons are required at the very least for each large fruit or vegetable plant, such as peppers, eggplants (Solanum melongena), tomatillos (Physalis philadelphica), dwarf blueberry bushes, cucumbers (Cucumis sativus), summer squash/zucchini (Cucurbita pepo), and bush-type winter squash varieties.

• A minimum of 5 to 8 gallons for each medium-sized vegetable or flowering plant, such as bush-type cucumbers, okra, broccoli, cauliflower, and cabbage (Brassica oleracea var. capital), as well as vars. botrytis, gemmifera, and Italica (Abelmoschus esculentus). This is also the recommended minimum soil volume for every ornamental grass or perennial with flowers or leaves that are included in a container.

- 1 to 2 gallons at the very least for each small-statured vegetable or flowering plants, such as spinach (Spinacia oleracea), lettuce, kale (Brassica oleracea var. sabellica), chard, collards, and other greens; as well as many flowering or foliage annuals.

This category includes individual herb plants as well.

- Roots and tubers like potatoes (Solanum tuberosum), carrots (Daucus carota subsp. sativus), beets (Beta vulgaris), radish (Raphanus sativus), onions (Allium cepa), and turnips (Brassica rapa subsp. Rapa) can be planted in almost any size container if the seeds or plants are spaced at the appropriate distance. But the fewer seeds or plants a pot can hold, the smaller it is.

Drainage

Adequate drainage is yet another crucial feature to look for in a container. Most garden pots sold in stores come with a drainage hole already drilled into the bottom, preventing excess irrigation water from soaking the soil and causing root rot and other problems. You will need to create a drainage hole yourself if the container you have lacks one already.

- To create a drainage hole in terracotta or concrete containers, use a drill equipped with a masonry bit.

- Use a drill with a tile bit if the container is made of glazed ceramic or glass.
- If the container is constructed of wood, use a spade or twist bit in your drill.
- If the container is constructed of metal, you can either drill holes through it with a high-speed steel (HSS) drill bit or use a scratch awl and hammer to punch holes through it.
- Use a spur-point bit or plastics drill bit if the container is composed of plastic or resin.

Drill through the bottom of the pot using a modest speed and constant, gentle pressure. Don't push too firmly or use the incorrect bit to prevent breaking the container. Instead of many small holes that are prone to clogging, it is preferable to create one or two sizable, 12- to 1-in.-diameter drainage holes in the bottom of a pot. Make each hole larger by rotating the scratch awl inside of it while drilling it with a hammer through the bottom of a metal container.

Drill through the bottom of the pot using a modest speed and constant, gentle pressure. Don't push too firmly or use the incorrect bit to prevent breaking the container. Instead of several little holes that are prone to clogging, it is preferable to create one or two sizable, 12- to 1-in.-diameter drainage holes at the bottom of a pot. Make each hole larger by rotating the scratch awl inside of it while drilling it with a hammer through the bottom of a metal container.

No feature of a container is more crucial than a place for extra water to drain.

A suitable drainage hole not only prevents the roots from resting in water but also permits more Salts from fertilizers will be removed from the soil by drainage water. Your plants' roots and shoot tips risk a salt burn from fertilizer if there is inadequate drainage.

After watering, empty the saucer if you're using it to catch drainage water that leaks out of the hole beneath your container. It's not much better to leave a saucer full of water under the plant than a pot with no drainage hole at all.

Materials

The type of material is the next aspect to consider when choosing pots for your container garden. An almost unlimited number of commercially produced garden pots are available, as well as an equal number of materials that can be recycled and transformed into growing containers. Before choosing which types of pots are a worthwhile investment, consider the advantages and disadvantages of each material.

Here are some of the most popular garden container materials, along with a list of things to think about before choosing one.

Terracotta/clay. Terracotta is heavy, breakable, and not weather resistant while being reasonably priced. Additionally, the exterior of clay pots may become stained with white salt and turn mossy green.

Contrary to a long-held misconception, putting rocks, broken pot chards, or other items in a pot's bottom that doesn't have a drainage hole doesn't "increase drainage" and it doesn't make the drainage any better. The opposite is true. The water table inside the pot will only rise if there are heavy materials added to the bottom, flooding the roots even faster. A proper drainage hole cannot be substituted with pot fragments or rocks.

Terra-cotta pots come in a wide variety of designs, sizes, and shapes, and those that have been burned and/or coated in the glaze are less likely to peel and crack. Because clay is porous, it dries out more quickly than other materials but gives roots good airflow. Clay also absorbs heat, which is great in the spring but bad in the summer when the soil temperature in the pot can rise too high.

painted ceramic. Glazed ceramic garden pots come in a variety of colors, designs, and sizes and are made from fine-textured clay that has been baked in a kiln and then coated with glaze. They are gorgeous, but they are also quite heavy, pricey, and breakable. Although these containers are less porous than bare terra cotta, they may withstand freeze-thaw cycles without cracking or flaking. Although the glaze is easily chipped, these containers are very decorative and hold moisture well.

Plastic. Over the past few decades, plastic garden pots have advanced significantly. To make the pots resemble other materials more, manufacturers increasingly add ornamental colors and designs. Plastic containers are cheap, lightweight, and considerably more resistant to cracking than terracotta or ceramic pots. Some plastic containers, which come in a variety of finishes, are vulnerable to fading, chipping, and breaking if dropped or left outside in the winter. Others have greater fortitude. All plastic pots effectively retain soil moisture, and double-walled plastic pots have good insulating qualities. To restore the appearance of faded plastic pots, paint them with high-quality exterior paint.

Wood. Half whiskey barrels have long been among the most popular garden containers, but they're not the only type of wood planters you can use. Planter boxes made of wood are inexpensive, especially if you're willing to build them yourself. Both cottage-style gardens and suburban landscapes benefit from the ca woods' casual, organic appearance really, the best planters are made of rot-resistant woods like redwood, cedar, or locust, though pressure-treated lumber can also be used in planters where no edibles will be grown. Even though wood planters will eventually need to be replaced, you'll use them for many years before that happens. Wood is a great insulator, shielding roots from temperature changes in the summer. Both in the summer and the winter. You can learn how to construct your wooden planter box in an upcoming project.

Resin. Most premium resin garden pots are created by "baking" a low-density polyethylene composite after it has been poured into a mold. To give, They might be fashioned to resemble granite, stone, or other materials to give them a modern appearance that is highly light, maintenance-free, and crack-resistant. Poor-quality resin planters may deteriorate over time if exposed to sunlight. Resin-based containers can withstand temperature changes well, and some brands use recycled materials.

Fiberglass. Fiberglass garden pots are strong and light, and they are frequently molded into a variety of designs and patterns to resemble concrete, stone, or glazed pottery. However, due to their fragile walls, they may break if dropped. They are also typically expensive. Glass fibers are woven into plastic to create fiberglass.

Fiberstone. Crushed limestone and fiberglass are blended with a composite to create this substance. Containers made of fiberstone have a stone-like appearance but are lighter and easy to transport. Fiberstone pots can be placed outside all year long and are less prone to fracture or flake since they are weather-resistant and have thicker walls than typical fiberglass planters. The major drawback is their high cost.

Metal. Copper galvanized metal, stainless steel, steel, cast iron, aluminum, and numerous more metals can all be used to make metal containers. Even if they are beautiful, some types, especially steel and cast iron, may rust if they are not painted. Aluminum and other thinner metals are lightweight yet quickly dent. among others

Although they are incredibly heavy, materials such as cast iron are unlikely to shatter or dent. Aluminum, galvanized metal, copper, and stainless steel are among the metals that may withstand rusting. Some brands of steel and aluminum can have a powder-coated finish that gives them a vibrant, fading-resistant appearance.

plastic foam. Despite being manufactured to resemble heavier materials like terracotta, stone, concrete, ceramic, or metal, high-quality polystyrene foam containers can be extremely pricey. Plant roots are adequately protected from extreme heat and cold by foam planters. Though their light weight is unquestionably a positive, these containers aren't as robust as some other materials. Containers made of polystyrene foam with raised or embossed decorations may chip or dent.

These pots can be used for a long time and left outside all year.

fabric grow bags/pots. These incredibly thin containers are constructed from a highly maneuverable, fibrous fabric called geotextile. Even some brands have handles. The best brands to look for if you're growing food are those that are BPA-free, and fabric pots are reasonably priced. Fabric bags' ability to avoid root circling and pot-bound plants is one of their main benefits. Instead of beginning to the circle inside the pot when a growing root hits the fabric, the root branches, generate a fibrous network of roots instead of a pot-bound plant. Even when left outside in the winter, the containers last for several years since the roots stay inside the fabric. Additionally, fabric pots permit efficient gas exchange, allowing the roots to breathe and regulating soil temperatures. They come in a wide variety of hues and dimensions; some are so large that you could even grow sizable trees in them.

Fiber-lined. This design, which consists of a metal frame lined with coconut fiber (known as coir) or a synthetic alternative that looks similar, is used to make a variety of containers, including porch planters, hanging baskets, hayracks, deck railing planters, and many others. Fiber-lined pots are attractive and reasonably priced, but they dry up extremely fast unless a thin piece of plastic with a few drainage holes is placed between the fiber and the potting soil. The fiber-lined planters' natural appearance makes it worthwhile to replace the liners every several years.

Concrete. Large concrete planters are virtually impossible to move despite being highly hefty and weather resistant. Concrete is typically thought to be quite inexpensive, although the price can vary substantially depending on the design and size of the container. Concrete pots get a lovely patina over time. As a great insulator, concrete will shield roots from extremely high or low temperatures.

Hypertufa. This sturdy, frost-proof substance, which is much lighter than concrete but has a comparable appearance, is a great substitute for concrete. It is relatively simple to manufacture hypertufa by mixing peat moss, perlite, a naturally occurring volcanic glass that is heated until it expands into smooth particles, and Portland cement (a special type of cement used to make concrete and stucco). To create your hypertufa planter, refer to the project that is discussed later in the text.

HOW BALCONY GARDENING SAVED MY MARRIAGE

Making Potting Soil from Scratch at Home

Making your potting soil is a great method to cut costs and may be customized to meet your specific needs. For large batches, use a cement mixer or a compost tumbler; for smaller ones, use a wheelbarrow, a large bucket, or a mortar mixing tub to combine the ingredients.

To get a consistent outcome, make sure to fully combine everything. Also keep in mind that if compost isn't already included in the recipe, you'll need to combine the finished product and compost until they are evenly distributed.

Mixture for general-purpose container gardening (With Compost Already Added)

6 gallons of coir fiber or sphagnum peat moss

14 cups of lime powder (if using peat moss) 4 12 gallons of perlite or vermiculite

Compost in 6 gallons

Add to a mixture: 12 cup bone meal, 14 cup kelp meal, 2 cups rock phosphate, and 2 cups green sand. To the completed mixture, add 112 cups of this fertilizer mixture. Alternately, you can substitute 112 cups of any granular, organic, complete fertilizer.

Container gardening mix from Soilless (Without Compost)

6 gallons of coir fiber or sphagnum peat moss Vermiculite or perlite in 6 gallons

Pulverized dolomitic limestone, 4 tablespoons

14 cups of bonemeal

Blood meal, 2 teaspoons

Mixed Perennial and Shrubs in Pots
1/3 of compost
1 component fine sand
Sphagnum peat moss, 1 component Pine bark composted in one part Perlite, one part
For each gallon of peat moss, add 1 tablespoon of lime.
potting mix for succulents and cacti
potting soil in 3 gallons (either a commercial brand or the homemade mix above, without compost)
two liters of fine sand Perlite, 1 gallon

Use the batch of homemade potting soil as soon as you can. However, if storage is required, put the mixture in plastic waste bags and keep them somewhere cool and dry. You may also spread the mixture on a tarp in a shed or garage and cover it loosely with a sheet of plastic.

The next project involves filling a recycled planter with unusual, drought-tolerant succulent plants using the cactus and succulent potting mix indicated above.

SUCCULENTS FROM CEMENT BIN
ESSENTIAL MATERIALS
A wheelbarrow with the handles and tire mount removed or an old cement mixing container filled to the brim with cacti and succulent potting soil
twelve to fifteen succulents
a couple of handfuls of rounded, decorative rocks

shells or other ornamental things (optional)

NEEDED TOOLS: Hammer, Eye protection with a scratch awl

In recent years, succulent plants have become quite well-liked, and for good reason. They require little upkeep, can withstand heat and drought, and are just stunning. Plants known as succulents hold water in their large, fleshy leaves. These plants are ideal for gardeners in arid locations or for people who occasionally "forget" to water because they can survive for long periods without water. These plants, however, don't fare as well in extremely humid climates or gardening regions with a lot of rainfall because they evolved in low-moisture environments.

Most succulents are not winter hardy, thus in some climates, they must be brought indoors in the fall before the first frost. In this project, a variety of succulent plants are grown in a recycled cement mixing bin using the specific cactus and succulent potting mix that was previously detailed.

The final chapter of this book contains a wealth of additional suggestions for using succulent plants in container gardens, in addition to this project (Chapter 6).

Several well-liked succulent plant options for a cement bin planter include:

Adromischus spp., Aeonium spp., Agave spp., Aloe spp., Crassula spp., Dudleya spp., Echeveria spp., Euphorbia spp., and Flapjacks (Kalanchoe thyrsiflora 'Flapjack') are a few examples of plant species.

Senecio mandraliscae, S. Serpens, Haworthia spp., Graptopetalum spp., Jade plants (Crassula ovata), Ox Tongue (Gasteria lilliputian), Portulaca spp., Sedum spp., Sempervivum spp., Sedum spp., Sedum spp., and others

HOW TO MAKE A SUCCULENT CEMENT BIN

STEP 1: Start by putting the empty bin in a spot that receives at least 6 hours of direct sunlight each day. Keep in mind that most succulents enjoy the heat. Once the bin is in position, use a hammer to make multiple holes with the scratch awl in the cement bin's bottom. To make the holes 12 inches in diameter, rotate the awl inside of them. Make the bin at least five or six drainage holes.

STEP 2: Add the well-draining cactus and succulent-specific soil mix described in the book's previous chapter to the bin until it is 2 inches from the top edge. Three gallons of potting soil, two gallons of coarse sand, and one gallon of perlite make up the mixture.

STEP 3: Plant the succulents in the container, taking special care to avoid any spikes or thorns. Because succulents are susceptible to rot when they are damp, position the plants such that there is the most airflow possible. Before planting the plants, make sure to gently release any roots that are circling inside the pot. Succulents shouldn't be planted too deeply.

The soil should be planted exactly as it is in the nursery containers. Their thick stems could rot if you plant them too deeply.

STEP 4: Top the soil with some decorative rocks, shells, and other accents, if desired, after all the plants have been positioned. Enjoy your new succulent planter and give the bin a good watering.

NOTE: Most of these plants are simple to propagate, so keep that in mind if you wish to enjoy more succulent plants in the future. Many plants spread using lateral growth; these young plants can be dug up, divided, and planted in other locations. It's also simple to grow succulents from stem or leaf cuttings. To learn how to grow plants from stem cuttings, refer to Chapter 5.

Your Containers Are Filled

Fill your containers with the 50/50 compost and potting soil mix using a soil scoop, shovel, or trowel. With larger plants, you might find it simpler to fill the pot 3/4 full, remove the plants from their containers, place them in the pot, and then fill in around them. The soil level after planting ought to be around 1 inch below the top rim of the pot. When filling your pots, keep in mind that even premium potting soil blends tend to settle a little after watering and throughout the growing season. The additional headroom at the top of the pot prevents irrigation water from evaporating and promotes its slow filtration through the soil to the roots of the plants.

Large containers that can carry a lot of potting mixes might be quite expensive to fill yet allow for larger plant root systems. Create a false bottom in larger pots by filling the bottom of the pot with huge, lightweight, chunky materials if you're trying to control your gardening budget. I've used drained milk jugs or cartons, empty soda cans and plastic bottles, upside-down buckets or flowerpots, plastic zipper-top bags full of Styrofoam packing peanuts, and empty soda cans and plastic bottles.

Make sure the items don't obstruct the drainage holes in the pot's bottom, and they shouldn't occupy more than 14 of the container's total volume. The roots of most plants will quickly spread out and encircle these objects. Using tiny and medium-sized pots does not require this practice. Only grow annual flowers, vegetables, tropical plants with only one growing season, or other short-lived plants using this kind of false bottom.

SETTING UP YOUR BOTTLES

Finding the ideal site for your container garden to flourish is the third and last pillar of the foundation for successful container gardening. Although there are several things to consider, sun exposure is arguably the most significant. Start by carefully observing your property for a while to determine how much sun each area receives during the day. Even though the sun tracks differently in the spring than in the summer or fall, a little observation can still reveal a lot. To confirm the light levels and sun exposure at different times of the year, you can also consult a website or smartphone sun-tracking app. The secret, of course, is to choose the ideal plant combination for the site's light exposure.

It is preferable to choose one of two approaches when

choosing a site. Either choose the plants you want to grow first, then place your containers in a location that will meet their lighting needs, or find a home for your containers first, then choose the plants for them based on the light conditions there.

For instance, choose a location that receives at least six to eight hours of full light each day if you want to grow plants that thrive in the sun, such as some types of blooming plants. If you don't have that kind of light, try switching to flowering or foliage plants, which thrive better in light shade, or move your containers around the house throughout the day to give them the most exposure to the sun. Growing in containers has many advantages, one of which is the ease with which lightweight, portable pots, a wheeled planter, or containers on pot dollies may be moved about to maximize light.

To offer the plants a few extra hours of light throughout the day, I am aware of numerous gardeners who move tomato and pepper containers from one side of the deck to the other as the day goes on.

Along with sun exposure, proximity to irrigation water is a crucial consideration when selecting a location for your container garden. The difficulty of transporting water-filled watering cans, buckets, or tubs to your garden is one of the biggest in gardening.

Plants in containers that are too distant from the spigot should be watered. Situate your container garden close to a hose to save yourself a lot of work.

After completing this unpleasant task and creating a sturdy

foundation for your container garden

It's time to shift gears and focus on picking the best plants for your pots and arranging them into lovely, productive plantings after picking the right kind of containers, filling them with the best potting mix, and selecting the ideal location for them.

CHAPTER TWO

How to Create and Plant Your Containers

It's time for the most enjoyable part of container gardening, plant choosing, and design now that the framework of your garden in containers is in place. Here, you can use color, form, and texture to convey your individuality. You can use vibrant combinations to catch the eye or monochrome combinations for plantings that will make a big impression. With a little skill, your container garden may be both useful and productive (particularly if you're growing vegetables!) while also serving as a location to showcase flair.

Before diving into container design, this chapter initially covers helpful advice for mixing various plant forms and sizes into a single planting. You'll learn how to use a few basic design concepts to arrange a variety of various plants into a harmonious arrangement.

Next, you'll learn about some of the top plants for container gardening in this chapter.

You'll be equipped with all the information you need to design and plant flower, vegetable, fruit, herb, and foliage containers thanks to tables and lists full of varieties adapted to container culture and a variety of growing situations. The chapter ends with a collection of photographs and "recipes" for foolproof containers that you may copy plant for plant or adapt to your own needs.

DESIGN OF CONTAINER 101

Good container design is a question of personal taste, just like decorating your home. There will be some color schemes that you like and some that you don't. The key is to discover your passion. But smart design goes well beyond color selection. Additionally, it involves combining vegetables, fruits, and herbs in a way that produces a good harvest as well as pleasing combinations of foliage and floral forms and textures. Additionally, choosing the appropriate container is just as important as choosing the right plants to combine.

HOW BALCONY GARDENING SAVED MY MARRIAGE

There are three main ideas to bear in mind when you develop your designs when it comes to planting lovely containers.

Proportion

Depending on which direction the designer erred, plantings that are out of proportion with their container appear off-balance, top-heavy, excessively dense, or flat. Proportion is crucial, even if your goal is to create a naturalistic container planting as opposed to one that appears planned.

The rule of thirds is a great tool for keeping proportion in floral design and container gardening. Start by examining the container's height. To maintain a pleasing ratio, your container should make up either 1 or 2 thirds of the combined height of the plants and container, with the remaining height coming from the plantings. In other words, you should aim for a 1:2 or 2:1 ratio between the height of the container and the plantings. The pot won't be exactly in proportion to the plant until it reaches its full height, but since most container plants grow quickly, it won't take long for that to happen.

Point of focus

Having a single focus point is another objective for the design of container gardens. A focus point might be overtly evident and direct or more covert. A fun focal point might also be based on a jazzy color, striking leaf textures, variegated foliage, or a narrow, vertical element. Usually, the largest plant in your design becomes a natural focus point by its size alone. Use only one primary focal point for each container, regardless of your decision. It can be quite distracting to have several focal areas.

Balance

Additionally, the vertical and horizontal balance of well-thought-out designs is always excellent. A container planting doesn't look top-heavy or unbalanced if it is balanced properly. A tree planted in a tall, narrow container will always appear to be on the verge of falling over because the visual equilibrium from top to bottom is incorrect. Alternatively, if you're using a window box or another long container, place the tallest plant in the middle or use two, at least three of them dispersed around the entire dimensions of the pot. But keep in mind that balance is not the same as symmetry. To achieve good balance, choose plants that are visually equal in weight to one another rather than using identical plants.

Here are five straightforward design guidelines that will assist you in putting together attractive plant combinations for your containers by combining proportion, focal point, and balance.

Style: Thriller, Filler, and Spiller

HOW BALCONY GARDENING SAVED MY MARRIAGE

The saying "Every container requires a thriller, a filler, and a spiller" is common among container gardeners. According to this idea, three plant heights should be used to fill out a container on every open plane while yet preserving balance and the right pot-to-plant ratio. This is a useful design strategy for containers that are intended to be viewed from all angles. By adhering to this guideline, you can guarantee that your design will look beautiful from all angles and won't have any "bald spots."

First, a single "thriller" plant is chosen for the pot's center. Typically, this is a big plant with striking leaves, intriguing flowers, or another attention-grabbing feature. To maintain the design appropriately proportioned, its mature height should fall within the limitations of the above-mentioned rule of thirds. There are many options for a thriller plant in nurseries; look for unusual plants that catch your attention and stand out from the crowd.

After choosing your thriller plant, search for "filler" plants to complement it. The thriller is surrounded by these plants, which fill in the space. Their mature height should be between a quarter and a half of the thriller film's height. Use three to seven filler plants, depending on the size of the pot. You can blend two or three distinct plant species into this layer, or they can all be of the same species. But beware of the "I-must-have-one-of-everything" traps; if you utilize too many different plants, this layer will become cluttered. Filler plants can be foliage, blooming, or a combination of the two. Numerous plants can be used as fillers in container plantings in both sun and shade.

The spiller plants are then positioned around the container's outer edge. These plants spill over the side of the container, covering them in eye-catching foliage or vibrant flowers. Spillers give the container a softer, more luxuriant feel. For each pot, I frequently use three different spiller plants—two flowering and one chosen for its intriguing vegetation Selecting too many will make the arrangement distracting.

Whatever plant species you use to fill each layer, make sure the scale is adequate for the container's size and that the plants are balanced both vertically and horizontally. Without going excessive, evenly distribute color, texture, and form across the container. Remember, choosing plants for their foliage texture and plant form as well as their flowers is just as important in creating a successful container garden design.

Style, Flat-backed

Containers that are intended to be seen only from one side and are snuggled up against a wall, fence, or pillar are ideal candidates for this design strategy. The flat-backed approach adds layers from back to front as opposed to

HOW BALCONY GARDENING SAVED MY MARRIAGE

using horizontal layers. This is one of my favorite container design strategies since it results in a styled planting when the appropriate plants are used in combination.

Start by choosing a tall, upright, narrow plant that meets the rule of thirds for the back of the container. Put it at the far back of the pot, a little off-center. Put this tall, narrow plant slightly to the left of the center in the back of one of the pots and then slightly to the right of the center in the other pot if you're designing two symmetrical, flat-backed planters to flank your front door, for instance.

Choose a little shorter plant to make up the second half of the back layer once you've planted the background plant. Compared to the first plant, this one should have more branches and be less upright. The back layer gains density while retaining some height. To complete your back layer in a large pot, pick two of these plants.

Create a second layer of plants immediately in front of the rear layer after selecting the back layer. They should be between one-half and three-quarters of the height of the back layer. The plants in this layer are a little shorter than those that make up the background. My favorite place to use plants is in the middle layer, where the foliage has interesting colors and textures.

Three foliage plants, each with complementary foliage

colors but different textures are combined in this middle layer of my favorite flat-backed containers. I frequently choose one with narrow, upright foliage, one with huge, dramatic foliage to act as the main point of the container, and one with soft, fine foliage. However, there is a lot of room for creativity here; the middle layer is also a wonderful place to add flowers.

At the front edge of the container, a flat-backed design's third and last layer is visible. It consists of one to three small-statured plants that, if desired, can cascade over the rim of the container. I try to use only one kind of plant in this layer to keep the composition from appearing cluttered, especially if you used a variety of plants in the mid-layer.

Do not maintain the plants in three exact rows while planting a flat-backed design. Instead, space the plants out, moving some slightly ahead or backward in each layer. By doing this, the planting gains depth and dimension while yet remaining well-balanced.

Each of the three layers in small containers planted in this manner can contain just one plant. But even with only three plants, this design produces a lovely result.

The style for the Featured specimen

This design strategy is the ideal approach to highlight a single, distinctive, tall specimen plant, such as a giant tropical banana, hibiscus tree, plumeria (Plumeria spp.), or possibly a tiny shade tree. The large-statured plant should be positioned in the exact middle of the container. To add the cherry on top, I like to surround it with complementary plants that don't overpower the focal point's attractiveness. These plants give the pot a heavier appearance, which helps to maintain my vertical equilibrium.

Low-lying plants that cascade over the edge of the container and form a ring around the base of the featured star make up this "icing" layer. Whether they are based on leaves or include flowers, the finest plants for this layer have a fine texture. Around the bold plant that takes center stage, I like to use plants with a light, frothy texture.

Monocultural Approach

In this type of container gardening, a single plant is used to fill the entire container. The container contains only one species, whether it be one plant or three to five of the same kind.

Each container is filled with a distinct plant, but all the plants complement one another by providing a single or complementary color theme, a balance of textures, or some other unifying aspect. I adore applying this approach with groupings of containers of varying heights. When there are three or more sizes of the same container, in my opinion, the monoculture style thrives. Although each plant is housed in a distinct container, the collection seems coherent.

Pay close attention to the plant's height while adopting the monoculture approach for container plants. If the pot-to-plant ratio is incorrect, it will be easy to see because every plant in the pot will be the same height.

Using Pot in Style

The final container garden design style disregards both the rule of thirds and a healthy pot-to-plant ratio. Using only extremely low or cascading plants in a container is known as the "pot-hugging" aesthetic. Though not for everyone, this design strategy results in some incredibly beautiful displays. Perhaps there is a large bowl of moss or a tall, rectangular planter with crawling plants in it.

Whatever plant and container combination you choose, the goal is for the plants to sit tightly against the container, whether it be ivy or a planter box filled with ground-covering succulents. People notice pot-hugging designs because they are unusual and make the entire container the focal point.

Always keep in mind that these are merely starting recipes as you design and construct your containers each year. With a little practice, you may improve upon these design strategies and customize them to suit your preferences. A good container garden design combines several factors, none of which should be taken too seriously. Avoid letting the demands of good design ruin the fun.

Using edible plants in the design

Fruits and vegetables grown in containers are frequently cultivated in a highly practical manner with little attention paid to the design and organization of the container. When it comes to container vegetable gardening, many gardeners tend to be more concerned with productivity than appearance, but they can have both function and form in one pot.

Fruit and vegetable plants in containers should also be attractive. Tomato plants don't need to be placed by themselves in a large pot. Vegetables can be grown in any of the five design categories, much like ornamentals. If you adhere to the advice given above, you'll have an attractive and fruitful edible container garden.

The thriller, filler, and spiller model, for instance, also applies to food plants. Large-statured vegetables like tomatoes, peppers, or eggplants can make for good thrillers. The suspense may alternatively take the form of an obelisk in the middle of the pot that is covered in pole beans or cucumbers, a fig tree, or even a blueberry bush. Plant chard, lettuce, bush beans, basil, and other greens nearby. Can use root vegetables like beets and carrots as the filler layer. Then, use spillers, such as thyme, strawberries, sweet potatoes (Ipomoea batatas), or cascading cherry tomato varieties, to fill in the outer edge of the pot.

You'll discover a listing of the top vegetable types for container culture later in this chapter.

Gardeners who grow vegetables in containers can also use a flat-backed version. Choose crops that meet each height niche and create layers for them in the same way that you would for ornamental plants. Columnar or dwarf fruit trees, huge tomato plants, figs, papayas (Carica papaya), citrus trees (Citrus spp.), bananas, a trellis of hardy kiwi vines (Actinidia arguta), or pole beans are all excellent food plant options for containers constructed utilizing the highlighted specimen style. Then, create a low-growing border around this focal point using a variety of herbs, lettuce and other greens, or edible flowers like nasturtiums (Tropaeolum spp.), marigolds (Tagetes spp.), and pansies.

When constructing edible container designs, it's crucial to take care not to overcrowd them. Vegetables require a lot of air movement to lower the risk of fungi illnesses as well as enough space to develop and produce at their peak. Don't overcrowd any one container with plants; instead, take your time to arrange them in lovely combinations. Pay close attention to the pot size recommendations provided in Chapter 1; doing so will enable you to decide how many vegetable plants to place in a specific container.

PLANTS YOU SHOULD SELECT FOR YOUR CONTAINER

Few activities are more fun than browsing the plant aisles of your favorite neighborhood nursery each spring. Every year, I buy plants for my container garden from five or six different garden centers since they all have different kinds of plants. I frequently have a list of must-have kinds based on research I've done during the winter, but I also frequently make impulse purchases, which over the years has resulted in some very eclectic containers—a behavior you may or may not want to imitate.

It makes sense that some individuals want to put the same things in their containers year after year to save time and because it is simple and comfortable. Others purchase prepared plant combinations and immediately start a container garden by planting them in containers. These are excellent choices, but don't be afraid to use your imagination by combining several new plants.

I've divided the likely plants you'll find at the garden center into eight different groups to help you in your endeavors:

Tropical plants, small trees, and shrubs, annuals for flowers and leaves, perennials, bulbs and tubers, vegetables and fruits for the backyard, herbs, and vegetables.

The best plants for each of these categories are listed in a chart after a brief introduction (except for backyard fruits). Each chart includes details on the ideal growing circumstances for the plant, as well as growth specifications and other important information, and is followed by a gallery of photos with other popular kinds. The backyard fruit category is quite complex, so a narrative rather than a chart will be used to present this section.

The succulents are one plant family that did not receive its category, nevertheless. Refer to the Cement Bin Succulent Planter project in Chapter 1 for suggestions on succulents.

You'll notice that the backyard fruit and vegetable parts are significantly lengthier than the others. This is because, when growing edible plants in containers, variety selection is far more important than it is for aesthetic plants. I also offer a list of varieties developed specifically for container culture in the vegetable section of the chart.

Flowers and foliage-producing annuals

A plant is considered annual if its entire life cycle is completed in a single year. In a single growing season, it sprouts, develops, blooms, produces seeds and then perishes. Annuals are common garden plants because most of them bloom for several months to spread as many seeds as they can before they die at the end of the growing season. However, many of the plants we grow as annuals are perennials that are sensitive to frost. For instance, coleus and fuchsia are perennial plants that cannot tolerate freezing conditions and are thus typically planted anew each year as annuals. The term annual is used in this text to refer to both true annuals and any perennials that are killed by the ice. Some of these plants may survive in your container garden for many seasons if you reside in a gardening zone where winter temperatures don't often drop below freezing. Chapter 5 provides advice on how to overwinter these frost-sensitive perennials indoors for gardeners in northern climates so you can keep them for many years as well.

Although adding annuals to your container plantings is frequently done to add flowers, you should also consider foliage-based annuals. These plants are attractive even when they are not in flower because of their distinctive foliage colors or leaf texture. Many gardeners clip or remove flower buds that are developing on these plants to emphasize their distinctive foliage even more. I try to incorporate at least one or two annual plants with leaves into each attractive container design. In addition to being beautiful and fascinating plants, foliage-based annuals might need less maintenance than their flowering relatives.

BEGONIA HANGING BASKET
ESSENTIAL MATERIALS

1 three-tiered hanging kitchen storage basket for fruit or vegetables

Burlap, natural, 1 yard (brown or light green)

Sheet moss, 1 small bag (available from a florist or craft store)

Fill all three stages with a 50/50 potting soil and compost mixture.

ESSENTIAL TOOLS: Scissors

This adorable, three-tiered hanging basket planter creates a distinctive presentation with a mix of foliage and flowering annuals. However, the technique recycles an existing set of hanging fruit or vegetable kitchen storage baskets rather than employing an expensive wire hanging basket. This inexpensive DIY alternative, which is styled in

HOW BALCONY GARDENING SAVED MY MARRIAGE

the same way as pricey coconut fiber-lined baskets is just as lovely.

Even though a variety of short-statured flowering plants

green annuals I put some shade-loving begonias in this planter along with some spiller plants that would spill over the sides.

The following plants are contained in this planter:

• Two Golden Creeping Jenny plants (Lysimachia nummularia 'Aurea')

5 mixed-foliage Rex begonias (Begonia rex hybrids), 1 trailing begonia for the top tier (I used Begonia 'Summer wings Rose'®), 1 English ivy (Hedera helix)

A HANGING Begonia Basket Making Instructions

STEP 1: To detach all three baskets from one another, start by detaching the chain hanger from the bottom two baskets. Next, set each basket on the burlap piece so that it is facing down. Cut a circle of burlap with scissors that are a few inches bigger than the rim of each basket.

STEP 2: Turn the baskets back over and line the interiors with pieces of sheet moss that cover the metal completely. Next, press the circle of burlap onto the moss.

To trim the extra, use scissors. The burlap can hang a little bit over the edge.

STEP 3: Reconnect the chain hanger to each of the baskets to replace it. Make sure the chains are positioned so that each basket is level before hanging the baskets from a shepherd's hook, tree branch, or ceiling hook. Each basket should be 3/4 full of the 50/50 potting soil mixture. Because begonias prefer shade, this basket will flourish best in a shady location or under a tree.

Step 4: Involves positioning the plants in the baskets such that the spillers are on the outside. There should be one spiller and two begonias in each basket. After all the plants are in position, add more potting soil around their roots.

Blend soil until each basket is filled, to within 1 inch of the top rim. Well-water each basket. Regular watering is preferred by Rex begonias, although they do not enjoy soil that is always wet. The baskets should be watered fairly frequently because the soil volume is so small, but Rex begonias are quite forgiving and will tolerate being left high and dry for a few days.

NOTE: This planter can be brought indoors and grown as a houseplant after the growing season is over and before the first fall frost. Rex begonias are beautiful indoor plants, but they want a greater humidity level than what is typically seen in houses. Hang your begonia basket, if you can, next to a bathroom window where the humidity from the shower will be beneficial. Rex begonias prefer bright, but not direct, sunlight indoors.

Perennials

Perennial plants are those that last for several growing seasons. While the root system typically survives the winter when the plant's top dies back to the ground, many perennials do keep some foliage that clings to the ground all year long.

In container gardening, perennials are a surprisingly valuable class of plants. Even though they often have a shorter flowering season than most flowering annuals, they give containers a distinctive look. Perennials are chosen for their ability to produce flowers or for the texture, color, and form of their foliage, much like annuals are. Hostas, coral bells, ferns, ornamental grasses, and spurges, perennials are grown primarily for their leaves and are ideal focus pieces and accent plants, especially when paired with complementing species, and plants in container designs.

Using perennials has several benefits, including the ability to be planted elsewhere in your garden after the growing season or to be grown in pots during the winter and used often throughout the year. Perennials also provide distinctive physical characteristics to the design.

Tubers and bulbs

Bulb-growing plants are another class of plants that do well in container gardening. Bulbs are floppy storage organs that are buried. Despite their biological differences, bulbs and tubers are frequently grouped as bulb plants, as I have done here.

The inclusion of both hardy spring and summer blooming bulbs as well as fragile tropical bulbs in pots is possible, but winter safety must be carefully considered. most people in northern climates, If the exterior of the pot is left out in the elements, potted flower bulbs won't survive the winter.

Even if the bulbs are winter-hardy at the time of planting. Hardy bulbs will, however, do quite well if you insulate the pots as instructed in Chapter 5 or relocate the pots to an unheated garage or root cellar that is cold but not freezing. On the other hand, tropical bulbs must be moved out of their pots and stored indoors in a dormant state or overwintered as houseplants. Summer-blooming and tender tropical bulbs are typically planted in the spring, while spring-blooming bulbs are usually planted in the autumn.

Because many of them are in bloom well before the weather is warm enough to plant annuals and warm-season vegetables, including pots of spring-blooming bulbs in your container garden, is a great way to add early-season color to your landscape. These bulbs can be removed from the containers once they have finished blooming and planted in other areas of the garden.

Caribbean Plants

Tropical plants are species that are indigenous to such areas. Tropical plants may be cultivated practically anywhere with the correct care, but they are best in warm, humid settings. Except in extremely warm locations, tropical plants are not winter resistant, and they frequently develop big leaves to maximize sunshine exposure. A lot of houseplants are leafy tropical that can survive and thrive indoors.

Many tropical plants have large leaves in addition to vividly colored flowers with strong fragrances or exotic forms and shapes, all of which were created by nature to tempt and entice very specific pollinators. Plants with distinctive characteristics abundant in tropical forests make excellent candidates for container gardens.

Tropical plants cost more than typical garden plants due to their beauty and rarity. These stunning plants are more expensive in greenhouses because they need special care, but if you're prepared to put in a little work, you can still grow them. Although most tropical plants cannot survive the winter outside, they can be easily overwintered indoors as houseplants or in a dormant state. I go into detail on how to do this in Chapter 5.

Tropical plants are ideal for featured-specimen and monoculture-style container designs because each one of these plants is large, bold, and gorgeous, though they also function well as the focal point in layered designs.

Smaller shrubs and trees

If you want to give your container plantings shade and structure, think about including tiny trees and shrubs in your ideas. a tree in a container or shrub provides height and makes a small balcony, patio, or deck appear larger while also offering shade and cover.

Smaller-statured trees and shrubs work well for container gardening. Avoid attempting to grow trees that get much bigger than 15 or 20 feet tall unless you have a very large container. And keep in mind that most containerized trees and shrubs require some root insulation when winter approaches, particularly if you live somewhere where winter temperatures often go below freezing. This kind of root insulation will also be covered in Chapter 5, but another choice is to take the tree or shrub out of its container after the growth season and plant it in the ground to ensure it survives the winter.

HOW BALCONY GARDENING SAVED MY MARRIAGE

Because they are such substantial design components, trees and shrubs work best when used in a highlighted specimen design approach.

Herbs

Plants grown for their flavor, aroma, or medicinal qualities are known as herbs. While some herbs are annuals that are sensitive to frost, others are perennials that come back year after year. Some herbs even resemble shrubs in their natural state. If planted at the appropriate temperature or the plants are overwintered indoors, some even develop into tiny trees.

Herbs used in cooking are excellent choices for container plants. Most plants are content to grow in pots, either on their own or in a mix of plants. Herbs can function in a container as a thriller, filler, or spiller depending on their structure and growth pattern. The foliage, flowers, stems, or seeds of the plant can all be used in cooking.

Although almost any herb may be grown in containers, some have been cultivated expressly to do so. The fifteen popular culinary herbs listed below are perfect for container planting. Most thrive best under circumstances of direct sunlight. In a container garden, many herbs serve two purposes: they can be used in cooking and, while in bloom, they draw pollinators and other helpful insects.

Harvest your herbs frequently to promote new growth and prevent blossoming (flowering sometimes alters the flavor). To cut sensitive fresh herb shoots or leaves for drying, use a sharp pair of scissors or pruners. If you choose to harvest whole shoots, bundle them up loosely and hang them up to dry for a few weeks in a cool, dry place. If you harvest individual leaves, you can dehydrate them for one to three hours in a food dehydrator. Or, to harvest chamomile, pull the little white and yellow flowers off with your fingers in a rake-like motion. Then, spread the flowers out on a cloth and turn them over once daily for 10 to 20 days to dry them. The easiest way to store dried herbs is to keep them out of direct sunlight and in airtight plastic or glass containers.

Vegetables

If you've ever wondered if you could grow your favorite vegetable in a container, the answer is yes—if you use the right plant and the appropriate container size. Vegetables with a tall stature require very large containers for optimum production. Additionally, the containers must be deep enough to accommodate the entire length of the mature roots if you are producing long, tapering root crops.

To combat fungal illnesses and promote growth, vegetables require enough air circulation, therefore picking the proper types is crucial. At the end of the season, you might be disappointed if you attempted to squeeze enormous vegetable plants into inadequate pots. Fortunately, there are a couple of solutions to this issue.

First, know that breeders have created smaller, bush-type kinds of practically all your favorites if you wish to produce vine harvests but lack the space. These veggies have been engineered to produce well from tiny plants, making them ideal options for container gardens. Bush cucumbers, watermelons, pumpkins, cantaloupes, winter squash, and summer squash are some of these smaller varieties. In the chart at the end of this section, I've listed my top picks for bush vine crop varieties.

Although tall, vining pea varieties and pole beans also thrive in containers, providing you provide them with a solid trellis, peas and beans also have varieties bred to have more compact growth. Numerous suggestions for making special trellises and staking systems for containers can be found in Chapter 3.

Miniature or patio-type vegetable varieties are also excellent for container gardening, in addition to bush-type vine crops. Tomatoes, eggplants, peppers, okra, and even sweet corn have all been designed specifically for containers, and more are being created every year. A smaller soil volume is needed for optimal growth because they are more compact, but they still yield a large crop.

Many other veggies come in dwarf and small-sized versions as well. Some were developed expressly for food, while others were grown to appear cute on a plate.

Container gardening works well with a miniature or patio-style vegetables kinds. These "French Breakfast" radishes and other cool-season crops enjoy the cool spring and fall weather.

The consideration of container growers. Unlike "baby" vegetables, which are just full-sized vegetables that have been picked early, these diminutive crops are not the same as those. Instead, even when fully developed, these are small miracles.

These little vegetables stand out in a container, from orb-shaped carrots, tiny lettuce heads, and pint-sized cabbages to tiny broccoli plants, dwarf kale, and beets no bigger than a ping-pong ball. Even dwarf types of Brussels sprouts exist!

Of course, not all vegetables grown in containers need to be dwarf or compact types. Numerous plants thrive in pots when grown in their natural state. Radishes, cauliflower, turnips, kohlrabi, chard, lettuce, spinach, onions, and tomatillos can all be grown in containers.

Timing needs to be considered in addition to the kind of plants to plant. While some vegetables are warm-season plants that cannot resist frost, others like the chilly spring and fall weather. Warm season

While cool-season crops tend to be planted either early or very late in the growing season, crops are best planted after the threat of frost has passed.

The contrasts between these two types of plants are explored in greater detail in Chapter 5, which also teaches you how to enhance yield by succession planting.

The preferred method of planting vegetables is a final factor to consider while growing them in containers. It's advisable to give some crops a head start by planting seeds indoors under grow lights or buying transplants from a nearby nursery because some crops take longer to mature.

Tomatoes, peppers, eggplants, and okra are a few examples of warm-season fruiting plants that are best cultivated from transplants that are already 6 to 8 weeks old. Cucumbers, pumpkins, melons, and other vine crops may also be started in the same manner by northern gardeners due to their shorter growing seasons. Direct seeding into a container is a simple way to begin growing vegetables.

Garden Fruits

Because not all backyard fruit kinds can withstand the strain of container growth, choosing the correct fruit varieties is crucial. You may find detailed instructions for creating a containerized berry garden with a mix of blueberries and raspberries after this section.

To produce fruit, apple trees require a partner for cross-pollination. You will therefore need to plant two distinct trees, each of a different kind. Alternatively, cultivate trees by grafting different species onto a single tree.

Strawberries are one option for fruits and berries grown in backyard containers, but there are many others.

Trees, shrubs, brambles, vines, and herbaceous plants are used to grow fruit in backyards. Let's examine each of them individually.

tree fruit

Although fruit trees are a wonderful complement to container gardens, not all fruits work well there. Except for citrus, most fruit trees need a certain number of chill hours below 45°F to effectively grow and bud. Be prepared to do some study to identify the precise types that need fewer chill hours if you reside in a warmer climate. For instance, whereas some apples only need 100 cold hours, others require well over 500. To prevent the trees from bursting out of dormancy too early in the north, look for varieties with a higher required chill hour requirement.

Fruit trees can be grown in containers of two different types: columnar and dwarf.

Miniature Fruit Trees

Look for dwarf or mini-dwarf options in the first place. Only dwarf or mini-dwarf kinds of apples, pears, peaches, and other fruit trees will work as container plants. Grafting fruiting buds from one fruiting variety onto a dwarfing rootstock (or root system) from another variety results in dwarf fruit trees.

Apples (Malus pumila) (Malus pumila). If you have a large enough container, any apple that has been grafted onto a dwarfing rootstock is a good candidate for container culture. However, apples grafted onto unique rootstocks like EMLA 27 and G65 known as Mini-dwarf apples are extremely productive despite only growing to a height of 4 to 6 feet. They are ideal for container gardening and tiny yards.

You'll need at least two different varieties of apple trees to ensure adequate pollination because apple trees are not self-fertile (meaning the pollen from one variety cannot fertilize the flowers of the same variety). Both varieties must be in bloom at the same time and be compatible with pollination partners. Lists of reliable pollinator partners are frequently provided by fruit tree nurseries.

Due to space constraints, you might choose to cultivate a combination tree instead of just one apple tree. Multiple apple types are grafted onto a single tree to produce these trees. One tree is sufficient because the various varieties work to pollinate one another. One of the varieties is found on every branch.

Pears (Pyrus communis) (Pyrus communis). Even dwarf types of pears can grow rather large, making them a poor choice for container gardens. However, if you can find a variety that has been grafted onto the Pyrodwarf rootstock, a specialized rootstock for dwarfing plants, your chances of success will increase. With one annual trimming, trees grafted onto these specialized rootstocks maintain a height of under 15 feet at full maturity. You'll need two or more trees, each of a different variety, as pears do bear fruit without a cross-pollination partner but do much better with a pollinator variety nearby.

nectarines with peaches (Prunus persica).

Among my favorite fruits for container gardening are these stone fruits. True genetic dwarf varieties perform even better in containers than standard grafted dwarf trees. They only grow to a maximum height of 5 feet, but they produce large fruits. Cherries and nectarines are self-fertile, so you don't need a partner for pollination, but the majority do need a lot of chill hours, so they're a

HOW BALCONY GARDENING SAVED MY MARRIAGE

A wonderful option for gardeners in colder climates. The peach varieties "El Dorado," "Pix Zee," "Honey Babe," and "Empress," as well as the nectarine types "Necta Zee" and "Nectar Babe," are a few great genetic dwarf variants. Due to their genetic similarity, nectarines and peaches can even be grafted onto the same tree.

Plums (Prunus spp) (Prunus spp). If you choose kinds produced on dwarfing rootstocks, plums are yet another fruit that works well in container gardening.

Additionally, combination plum trees are extremely common; some even come with other stone fruits like peaches and apricots. For the finest height control, look for plums that have been grafted onto a dwarfing rootstock and be ready to prune them annually.

juicy cherry (Prunus avium).

If you prune them correctly, cherry varieties are grown on dwarfing rootstocks, like Gisela 5 and 3, meaning you don't have to climb a huge ladder to harvest cherries. These trees only require one annual pruning and reach a height of between 10 and 12 feet. grafted cherries on New Root 1 Zaiger rootstock only reach heights of 6 to 8 feet. When selecting which cherry types to grow, keep in mind that while most tart cherries (P. cerasus) are self-fertile and don't require another variety for pollination, most sweet cherries (but not all) will need another variety for cross-pollination. Multiple types of cherries are grafted into combination cherry trees. Most cherry trees need a lot of chill hours, so northern gardeners can also grow them well. As a self-fertile sweet cherry that is great for containers, "Syliva" is a great dwarf cherry to keep an eye out for.

Pomegranate (Punica granatum) (Punica granatum). It is possible to grow this lovely plant as a tiny tree or bush. Pomegranates are only hardy down to about 10°F, so they grow best in the southern United States and California where they produce delicious fruit and lovely foliage. Pomegranates can easily be pruned to preserve a short stature and are self-fertile. The superb dwarf cultivars "Red Silk" and "Parfianka" thrive in pots.

Fruit-bearing Plants

Shrub-borne fruits provide excellent choices for container gardens as well. These backyard fruits are great complements to edible container gardens, even though there are fruiting bushes that can get large if you keep a look out for kinds with a shorter growth habit.

Blueberries (Vaccinium spp) (Vaccinium spp.)

Blueberries are great for container growth due to their shallow, fibrous root systems; however, certain kinds do

HOW BALCONY GARDENING SAVED MY MARRIAGE

better than others.

For container gardeners, this involves adding an acid-specific granular organic fertilizer to the potting soil before planting. Blueberries grow best in slightly acidic soil. For information on how much fertilizer to add, refer to the label (more on container fertilization in Chapter 3).

Some types of blueberries can endure temperatures as low as -35°F, and they flourish best on acidic soils with a pH range of 4.0 to 5.0 and full to partial light. Blueberries come in a variety of varieties, including high-bush, low-bush, rabbit-eye, half-high, and a variety of other hybrids.

Growing half-high variants, which mature to a height of 3 to 4 feet, or miniature types is recommended for container gardeners.

There are a few self-pollinating, small blueberries that are ideal for container gardens, but most blueberries need two or more kinds to get maximum pollination and fruit production. In most gardening zones, "Top Hat," "Jellybean," and "Blueberry Glaze" are good choices for pots because they only reach heights of 18 to 24 inches.

The rabbit-eye variety is your greatest option if you live in the south because they thrive in regions with warm winters. For southern container gardeners, the 3-foot-tall Sunshine Blue' is a fantastic option; while it is self-fertile, it performs best when cross-pollinated with another plant.

Although it only grows to a height of 18 inches, the mid-season ripener known as "Northsky" is a favorite in the northern hemisphere. However, it does require cross-pollination with another variety.

Gooseberries (Ribes hirtellum) (Ribes hirtellum)

The container garden is delighted to have these unusual fruits there. Choose one of the many sweet gooseberry options instead of the many tart-flavored kinds, such as "Jeanne," "Black Velvet," "Poor man," and "Amish Red." They can endure winter temperatures as low as -40°F and can thrive anywhere outside the very hot southern regions. Gooseberry shrubs grow to a height of 2 to 4 feet and bear a lot of berries. Even though a lot of gooseberry bushes have spines, thornless types are preferable.

Currants (Ribes spp) (Ribes spp.)

The mature height of this charming little berry bush is only 3 to 5 feet. Currants can withstand temperatures as low as -40° F and are generally disease- and pest-resistant.

Although most currants are self-fertile, they all offer greater results when grown in combination with other varieties. The flavor of some current kinds can be rather tart, making them unsuitable for fresh consumption, but they work wonderfully in jams, jellies, sauces, and syrups.

Currants come in a variety of stunning hues, such as red, black, white, and pink, and are generally good

HOW BALCONY GARDENING SAVED MY MARRIAGE

producers throughout most of North America—except in areas where winter temperatures drop below -40° F or where summer temperatures are extremely hot. However, due to the plant's capacity to act as a vector for white pine blister rust, planting various currant and gooseberry varieties—specifically, black, red, and white currants—is prohibited in several areas. Please be mindful of any limitations in your state.

Figs (Ficus carica) are delicious fruits that grow well in containers. Because the plants can be readily brought indoors for the winter, container culture is ideal for figs even in the north where they must be carefully overwintered.

Depending on the way the plant is pruned, figs can be grown as either a tree or a shrub. Numerous fig varieties exist, some of which have incredibly specialized climatic demands. Speak with other local fig growers, or stick with more hardy kinds like "Excel," "Hardy Chicago," "Petite Negri," "Brown Turkey," "Black Mission," and "Norland."

FIRST-TIME BERRY GARDEN
ESSENTIAL MATERIALS
Galvanized metal utility tub, 6 or 28 gallons
Fill the tub with a 50/50 potting soil and compost mixture.

1 cup of granular fertilizer made especially for plants that love acid

a blueberry bush

ten to fifteen strawberry plants

Awl for scratching, a hammer, Eye protection

Berries don't require a lot of space to grow. In this container planting, blueberries, and strawberries—two of the most well-liked little fruits—are combined. Even though the two require slightly different soils (blueberries prefer a more acidic environment), they both thrive in a mixture of peat-based potting soil, compost, and acid-specific fertilizer. If you reside in an area where temperatures frequently drop below freezing, a little additional care will be needed to keep this container over the winter.

Blueberries don't require a particularly deep container to grow because of their vast, shallow, fibrous root systems. Galvanized utility tubs are therefore ideal containers for producing blueberries.

HOW TO CREATE A BERRY GARDEN FOR A BEGINNER

STEP 1: Turn the metal tub over and use the hammer to pound drainage holes into the bottom of the metal tub in six to eight different locations. The potting soil mixture should be poured into the tub to within an inch of the upper rim. Make sure to evenly distribute the cup of granular fertilizer made specifically for acids in the growing mixture.

STEP 2: In the middle of the tub, place a single blueberry bush. Selecting a blueberry variety with care is important because not all of them grow well in containers. Find a blueberry variety that has been bred to thrive in containers for the greatest results. Greater variations will quickly fill the available space. Northern climates are ideal for self-pollinating miniature blueberry types with a height of 18 to 24 inches, like "Top Hat," "Jelly Bean," and "Blueberry Glaze." Use a rabbit-eye kind of blueberry in southern climates instead (just plan on planting two berry tubs because rabbit-eyes are not self-fertile and need a pollination partner).

STEP 3: Arrange ten to fifteen strawberry plants, spaced three to six inches apart, around the base of the blueberry bush. Select an ever-bearing variety if possible, that will deliver a continuous crop of fruit from early summer to fall. Also, keep an eye out for types that naturally resist illness. Throughout the growing season, give the plants plenty of water and care. For container-grown strawberries, it's all right to let the plants produce fruit during their first season; some people advise pinching off all the strawberry flowers during the first growing season to strengthen the plant roots.

NOTE: It's vital to surround your metal berry tub with a ring of chicken wire or cattle fencing that is approximately 2 to 3 feet wider than the tub and the same height when winter hits to give it a little extra protection. To insulate the roots, place some straw, hay, or autumnal leaves between the tub and the fence. Avoid covering the top of the tub or the plants because doing so could unintentionally encourage the spread of fungi. In the following season, 4 to 6 weeks before the last anticipated frost, remove the fencing and insulation materials. When the fencing is taken down, you should fertilize the area once more annually with 12 cups of granular, acid-specific fertilizer.

Concerning Fruit Pollination

Even if you've followed all the instructions, if your plants flower profusely but don't produce fruit, inadequate pollination is likely to be at fault. Make sure you have the right pollination partner for your plant to start fixing the issue. Keep in mind that many fruits are not self-fertile, and that fruit production will be very low or nonexistent in the absence of another variety with which to exchange pollen. Most fruits also need insects to transport pollen from flower to flower, and some plants are extremely dependent on specific pollinators. Bumblebees, for instance, are great at pollinating blueberries. Include a lot of flowering plants in your container garden to attract lots of pollinators. Plant several annuals, perennials, herbs, and other pollinator-attracting flowers all around fruit trees, bushes, vines, brambles, and herbaceous fruits that are grown in pots. You can grow more fruit if there are more pollinators nearby.

CONTAINER PLANTATION

After carefully choosing your plants for your containers and adding dirt to your pots, it's time to start planting. To start, arrange your plants first, then plant them.

Before planting, leave the plants in their nursery pots and put them on top of the soil; this enables the plants to be moved and rearranged. Before deciding where to place each plant, check the maturity height of all the types by reading the pot tag or doing a web search. Keep a specific design style in mind as you move the plants around, and after you're comfortable with where they are, begin the planting procedure. Carefully place one hand over the top of the container when removing a plant from its nursery pot, then wrap your fingers around the stem on each side. Turn the pot over using the other hand, then use a gentle knock to remove the soil and roots into your waiting hand. Examine the roots of the plant after it has been removed from its nursery pot. Before planting, loosen them if they are circling inside the pot.

If this step is skipped, the roots won't expand into the soil and fill their new, larger home; instead, they will remain rolled up in a ball.

Use your fingers, a soil knife, or a trowel to carefully peel apart the root mass's outer layer to release roots that are encased in pots. Don't be afraid to tear any of the larger roots as well as some of the finer root hairs. This just promotes a more branching root system, which will expand into the potting soil more quickly. You might require a pair of pruning shears or perhaps a tiny folding saw to free the roots if they are very tightly tied to the pot.

Each plant should be planted at the same depth as when it was in its nursery pot. As you plant, you might need to add additional dirt to the container or remove some soil to make a place for all the plants.

If you're directly sowing seeds into pots, check the seed packet first to find out how far apart to space them, how deep to plant them, and when to sow them.

After everything has been inserted, properly water the container. Add a little more potting mix to the top if you notice that the soil has settled too much, exposing the tops of the root balls or settling much lower than the upper rim of the pot. Just be careful not to pile the soil up around the plant stems or you run the risk of girdling the plants.

CHAPTER THREE

Maintenance of Your Containers

In any type of gardening, it's crucial to keep in mind that plants are surprisingly forgiving. A little tree with sliced branches will look great once it is properly trimmed, and a perennial that was forcibly cut back by an enthusiastic gardener will swiftly outgrow even the worst "haircut." Rhododendrons that have been pruned into weird shapes will eventually outgrow their odd shapes. In a garden, there aren't many faults you can make that can't be fixed.

I'm going to give a lot of plant maintenance and care advice in this chapter, but you should be aware that none of it is set in stone. Yes, if you complete every job listed in this chapter, your container garden will undoubtedly be beautiful, healthy, and productive, but you won't necessarily suffer the consequences if you occasionally omit a few of them. Make every effort to take good care of your containers, make mistakes, and learn from them. If something doesn't work out, just try again the following year.

But even if you occasionally can omit some of the following upkeep duties, there is one that you simply must not omit when it comes to container gardening. And since this one fundamental responsibility is so important, we'll start by discussing it.

WATERING

Most container-grown plants that don't thrive are a result of the gardener either forgetting to water them or watering them incorrectly. There is no question that the plants must receive regular and constant watering if you want a lovely container garden.

How often?

A container's irrigation requirements are directly correlated with the amount of potting soil it holds. Smaller containers require more frequent watering; if a small clay pot is exposed to direct summer sunlight, you may need to water it twice or three times daily. The larger the pot, the less frequently you'll need to water it because the larger volume of potting soil found in larger containers can store more moisture.

There are additional elements to consider because watering requirements vary depending on the size and variety of plants. Bigger plants require more water, regardless of the size of the container they are growing in (unless, of course, you are growing a cactus or another plant with minimal water requirements). Additionally, adult plants typically require more water than young ones do.

This means that when the season changes and the plants enlarge, a container often needs increasing amounts of water. Porous containers, such as planters lined with moss or unglazed clay, tend to dry out more regularly Choose glass, glazed ceramic, plastic, metal, or fiberglass containers over terracotta if you want to reduce how frequently you must water.

Rainfall also has an impact. Invest in a rain gauge and bury it in one of your containers at the soil level or just above. The quantity of precipitation that reaches that location will be gathered and measured.

However, be aware that rain may slip off vegetation and bounce back, diverting it from where it is needed. Even after a heavy downpour, you might find your rain gauge empty because the leaves scatter the raindrops before they reach the soil. The only sure way to be sure is to go outside and physically check the moisture content of your pots.

There are numerous methods for determining a container's moisture content. You have three options: feel the weight of the pot, wait for the plant to wilt, or buy a fancy moisture sensor meter or soil water monitor to insert into the soil. But sticking a finger into the pot until it reaches your knuckle is the most accurate approach to measure the amount of soil moisture. Water the soil if it is dry. Don't if it isn't. Furthermore, you won't ever need to worry about overwatering because any extra water simply drains out the hole in the bottom of the pot if you did a good job choosing a pot with adequate drainage. This brings us to the following point of consideration.

The amount?

Another error is to irrigate using the "splash-and-dash" technique, which involves spritzing each plant with water in the morning and possibly splashing some on the ground as you go. Water is sprayed on the leaves, while the roots are left dry. The plants suffer, and the gardener is baffled as to why the plants in their containers aren't flourishing despite "watering them every day."

For in-ground gardens or lawns, this "splash-and-dash" irrigation method, where a small amount of water is added each day, is also bad. The entire root system of plants requires deep, comprehensive irrigation that permeates through the soil. Deep irrigation encourages deep, self-sufficient root systems, whereas shallow irrigation encourages shallow root systems that cannot access sufficient nutrition or withstand any amount of drought. This means that when using containers, you must apply irrigation water directly to the root zone and repeatedly soak the soil until at least 25% of the applied water drains out the drainage hole in the bottom of the pot.

WATERING

Most container-grown plants that don't thrive are a

result of the gardener either forgetting to water them or watering them incorrectly. It is a fallacy to claim that frequent, light watering prevents overwatering, applying water too frequently leads to overwatering. The inability of the roots to breathe when the soil is perpetually moist causes the plant to wilt and eventually die. Unfortunately, the signs of overwatering and underwatering are very similar.

Balance is the key to effective container irrigation. Water your plants as often as necessary but try to give them plenty of water. Between waterings, let the growing medium dry out a little bit, but not so much as to stress the plants.

Set a reminder on your smartphone if you're concerned that you'll forget to check the moisture levels of your containers. Alternatively, if you don't have the time to frequently check for irrigation needs, think about growing your container garden in self-watering planters, such as the commercial brands covered in Chapter 1, or by building the DIY self-watering planter shown in the following project sidebar.

Patio self-watering container
ESSENTIAL MATERIALS
2 identical-sized and kind plastic storage containers
1 vintage towel made of cotton enough to fill one of the bins with a 50/50 potting soil and compost mixture.
dated blocks or bricks Plants

TOOLS REQUIRED

Knife-utility, Work gloves, Scissors

It costs a lot of money to buy premade self-watering containers, especially if you need more than one or two. You may create five or six self-watering containers using the following step-by-step instructions for less money than it would cost to buy one. To grow tomatoes, zucchini, and other large vegetables, use large 50-gallon storage bins like those in the pictures. For smaller plants or spaces, choose smaller bins. Any size pair of plastic storage containers can be converted into a low-cost, self-watering planter by simply following the steps.

A Self-Watering Patio Container: How to Make One

STEP 1: Cut a 2-inch square hole at the center of the bottom of one of the storage bins using a utility knife. Cut the cotton hand towel lengthwise into four roughly equal-width strips.

STEP 2: Place the second bin where you want your planter to go. Next, fill the bottom of the second bin with columns of bricks or blocks that are 4 to 8 inches high to serve as a water reservoir. Make three brick columns for larger bins; for smaller bins, only two columns are required. Avoid placing a column exactly in the center of the bin because doing so can impede water flow. Utilize the tool to make a 2-inch square hole in the rear of this container, use a knife. Your brick columns' tops should be the same height as the top of the hole. The water reservoir will be filled into this hole, which will also act as an overflow outlet.

STEP 3: Pour water into the reservoir until it reaches the fill/overflow hole's bottom. As you nestle the first bin into the second, make sure the bottom of the interior bin is resting on top of the brick columns.

STEP 4: Gather the hand towel strips together and thread one end through the inner bin's bottom hole. The towel should extend through the hole far enough to touch the reservoir bin's bottom. Then, spread the upper half of the towel strips out into the container's bottom in the shape of a "+". As a wick, the towel strips will draw water from the reservoir and transfer it to the soil in the upper bin.

STEP 5: Fill the inside bin with a 50/50 blend of compost and top-quality potting soil. Keep the soil mixture from being overfilled; leave 1 inch of headroom at the top to catch any rainfall. You can now plant. Two patio-style bush tomatoes, two basil plants, a cucumber vine, a miniature watermelon vine, and a hot pepper plant will all be housed in this 50-gallon self-watering planter. Your plant list will need to be condensed if you utilize smaller bins. After planting, water the plants. You won't need to water from the top again after this.

Step 6: If necessary, insert cages and stakes. To support the tomato plants as they grow in this example, we utilized two colored tomato cages, but you could also use any of the trellising concepts covered later in this chapter.

STEP 7: Even while you won't need to fill the reservoir

every day, you do need to check it sometimes. By placing a hose into the hole in the back of the planter and letting it run until water begins to emerge from the hole, you may fill the reservoir. Depending on how empty the reservoir was when you started, you may require water.

The System for Delivering Water

The only thing that matters is that the water is directed toward the root zone of the plants rather than the leaves. There is no one optimum approach to giving water to your container garden. Many lovely container gardens are irrigated manually with water from watering cans, buckets, or pitchers. Others are watered by hand using a soft spray from a hose's end-mounted water wand nozzle. Consider installing an automatic irrigation system to water your containers, though, if you want to reduce the time you spend watering.

If you grow a lot of fruits and vegetables in containers or if you grow for a living, this method is especially helpful. Drop-by-drop water is given to containers using automatic irrigation systems, which is particularly effective since the water is fed directly into the pot with very little water lost to evaporation or improper application. This kind of system is often built by running irrigation tubing down rows of containers and then extending a short segment of flexible tubing into each pot. Nursery, farm supply, specialty greenhouse, and irrigation supply firms all provide irrigation kits. Alternatively, you can build your automatic irrigation system by following the detailed instructions in the sidebar for the following project.

Irrigation systems can be installed and then connected to a timer, or they can simply be turned on and off by turning the spigot to which they are attached.

CONTAINER IRRIGATION SYSTEM MADE AT HOME

ESSENTIAL MATERIALS

1/4-in. black micro poly tubing, 1/2-in. poly irrigation tubing, and 1/2-in. poly tube end caps or the shut-off valve

6 basket-covered dripper stakes or 6 miniature in-line drippers

One drip irrigation faucet connection kit for 1-inch tubing, six 1/4-inch double barbed connections, and one programmable hose timer (optional)

TOOLS REQUIRED

Scissors, Measurement tape 1/4 in. irrigation tube hole puncher

This DIY irrigation system can water up to six pots at once, but you may modify the design to suit your needs by adding more tubing, dripper stakes, or branches, or even by using T couplings to add more pots. Commercial drip irrigation kits come with everything you need to build a similar system but building the system from scratch is more cost-effective.

A DIY container irrigation system construction guide

STEP 1: Place every pot that you want your irrigation

system to water in its designated location. Calculate how much 1-inch black poly irrigation tubing you'll need to install a line of pots from the closest pot to the farthest pot. Use a pair of sharp scissors to measure the tubing and cut it to size.

STEP 2: Add a shut-off valve or a poly tube end cap to the end of the tubing that is furthest from the hose spigot. Make sure the shut-off valve is in the closed position if you use one. To the end of the tube closest to the hose spigot, fasten the faucet connection kit. (You must extend the length of the garden hose from the spigot out to the faucet connection kit after assembling the system.)

STEP 3: Add lengths of microtubing line into each container at this point. Punch a tiny hole through the 12 in. black poly irrigation tubing you've set out with the hole puncher. For each drip line that will branch off the main line, drill a hole.

STEP 4: involves inserting a 1/4-in. double-barbed connector into each hole once it has been punched. With a little slack in each line, measure and cut a piece of 1/4-in. black micro poly tubing to extend from each barbed connector to the container. Over the exposed end of the double-barbed connector, slide one end of the micro-poly tubing down.

STEP 5: Push the other end of each micro poly tubing down over the nipple to attach a dripper stake with a basket or a small in-line dripper. If you're using micro in-line drippers, lay the end of the dripper on top of the soil instead of inserting the dripper stake with a basket into the soil of the container.

STEP 6: Turn on the faucet and attach your system to a hose to test it. By twisting the top of the basket, you might be able to regulate the amount of water flowing out of the dripper stakes you used. You should carefully inspect the system for leaks and fix any you detect.

STEP 7: If you'd want to regulate when and how much water is provided, attach a programmable timer to the spigot. Depending on your water pressure and how many pots are being watered on the same line, it may take some time to completely irrigate your pots. Run tests periodically to establish how long the timer should run for the containers to get all the water.

STEP 8: Disconnect your new irrigation system from the spigot before it gets too cold if you want to see it safely through the winter. Completely drain the system, then remove it from the ground and store it for the winter in a garage or shed. Alternatively, if you intend to leave it in place, blow air through all the lines to ensure that there is no moisture left inside of them using an air compressor.

TIP: Connect this DIY system to a tiny submersible pond pump to utilize it with a rain barrel (a 250- or 400-gallons-per-hour pump should work just fine). Plug the pump in after submerging it in the rain bucket. To water the pots, the pump will draw water from the barrel and send it through the irrigation tubing. A more potent pump will be required if you need to move the water uphill.

FERTILIZING

Beautiful as they are, garden malls and nurseries may

be very perplexing. Your mind will spin at the variety of fertilizers available on endless shelves and end caps.

A plant fertilizer is, by definition, a substance that is either a synthetic chemical or a natural substance that is put into soil or a growing medium to improve fertility and promote plant development. There has been a significant change in thinking over the past ten years, even though your mother may have watered her potted plants with a water-soluble chemical fertilizer every week. The notion of "feeding the plants" has given way to the notion of "feeding the soil."

By feeding the soil's living organisms, naturally generated fertilizers give your plants a much more well-balanced nutrient source that supplies mineral sustenance for developing plants. These tiny creatures break down these fertilizers into the nutrients that plants need to develop, the majority of which are fungi and bacteria. Additionally, a lot of these bacteria coexist advantageously with plant roots, giving plants specific mineral elements in exchange for trace amounts of carbohydrates. Our plants flourish when we nourish the soil.

Since the root system is contained in a tiny space, you might think that none of these matters for container gardening. However, if you use a 50/50 mixture of compost and potting soil to fill your containers, the exact opposite is true. Your compost is alive with helpful soil organisms in your containers. Additionally, compost has a variety of macro- and micronutrients that are crucial for plant growth.

Even when plants are grown in containers, science has demonstrated that fostering healthy, biologically active soil is the greatest method to encourage optimum plant growth.

However, there are occasions when our plants grown in containers require additional nutrition, such as when the nutrients in the compost are exhausted or unavailable. Several simple-to-use organic fertilizers are great at feeding the soil that may be used in those situations. These fertilizers can easily be added to containers during the growing season and are made from various combinations of naturally occurring materials. The fact that many of these natural fertilizers contain trace nutrients, vitamins, amino acids, and plant hormones that are sometimes absent from chemical fertilizers and aren't typically indicated on the label is an additional advantage of utilizing them. These substances play a crucial role in the health and vigor of plants by acting as natural growth promoters.

Looking at the Label

Spend some time reading the labels when purchasing fertilizers. There are four basic constituent sources for natural fertilizers.

1. Plant products. These are plant-based fertilizer constituents. Alfalfa meal, cottonseed meal, kelp meal, and corn gluten meal are a few examples.

2. Materials made of dung. On the label of natural fertilizer, you might also see pelletized chicken dung,

dried cow manure, cricket excrement, bat guano, and worm castings or worm "tea."

3. Byproducts from animals. These types of fertilizers frequently come from waste products produced by the food industry. Fish emulsion, bone meal, feather meal, blood meal, and crab meal are a few examples of what they consist of.

4. Minerals mined. Mined minerals like greensand, rock phosphate, crushed limestone, and potash sulfate are examples of natural fertilizers for plants.

When soil nutrients become depleted and adding more compost is not an option, using fertilizers made of a combination of these ingredients is a fantastic way to feed your soil.

But it's crucial that you comprehend the numbers on the package before selecting any kind of fertilizer for your container crop. Natural fertilizers include a statement about their N-P-K ratio anywhere on the bag in addition to their ingredient list. The percentages of the three macronutrients—nitrogen, phosphorous, and potassium—by weight are shown in this ratio. A bag of 10-5-10, for instance, has 10% N, 5% P, and 10% K. Filler products make up the remaining 75% of the bag's weight. The N-P-K ratio values for fertilizers with a natural composition are frequently lower.

This is because many of the nutrients in natural fertilizers are not immediately available after application; rather, it takes some time for the soil microbes to process these nutrients and release them for plant use. Label percentages are based on levels of nutrients that are immediately available. Although this could seem like a drawback, natural fertilizers act as slow-release fertilizers by gradually releasing their nutrients.

Understanding how plants use these various macronutrients is also crucial.

The chlorophyll molecule contains nitrogen, which supports healthy shoot and leaf growth. A fruiting or flowering plant, such as a tomato or a petunia, will experience excessive green growth when fertilized with a high nitrogen fertilizer (such as 6-2-1 or 10-5-5); this is frequently at the expense of the development of flowers and fruits. However, putting it on a plant that produces green, leafy vegetables like spinach or lettuce makes a lot more sense.

On the other hand, phosphorus is necessary to produce new plant tissue and the division of cells. It aids in the production of fruit and flowers as well as healthy root development. Phosphorus is crucial for promoting the growth of flowers and fruits as well as root crops including beets, carrots, and onions. Due to the high phosphorus content of both bone meal and rock phosphate, these fertilizers are frequently suggested for use on root crops.

Potassium controls the stomata, or gas-passing pores on a leaf's surface, which assist activate specific plant enzymes and regulate a plant's uptake of carbon dioxide. A plant's resilience and vigor are influenced by its potassium levels.

Planning

You have two main options when it comes to natural fertilizers for your container garden, which should make your decision easier. Let's discuss each of them individually.

Blends of complete granular fertilizers

Complete granular fertilizer mixtures come in dozens of different brands. The majority contain a variety of substances derived from plants, animals, and minerals, and depending on the brand, they may have an N-P-K ratio of 4-5-4, 3-3-3, or something akin. They are considered "complete" because they include a variety of components that offer some of each of the three macronutrients, as well as numerous trace nutrients, vitamins, and other substances. Make sure to select the right product for the plants you are cultivating because all of these have various formulations and compositions. Some full granular fertilizer blends are even designed and labeled for crops, such as tomatoes, flowers, or bulbs.

Follow the recommendations on the packaging when adding granular fertilizer to your containers for the best results. Many gardeners discover that treating their pots with granular fertilizers twice or three times during the growing season gives them the finest results.

It's possible to consume too much of a good thing with granular items. Even natural fertilizers can be overapplied without difficulty, which can result in nutrient deficits, a pH imbalance, or fertilizer "burn" (yes, even some natural fertilizers are capable of this). Avoid applying too frequently or in excess to avoid these problems. Once more, make sure to adhere to all label directions.

Flowing fertilizers

Both the roots and the foliage of plants absorb liquid fertilizer products. In general, plants can utilize nutrients that are given to them in a liquid solution more quickly and easily. Water soluble fertilizers, like other fertilizers, give plants some of the nutrients they need for greater yields, better development, and vitality, but not all liquid fertilizers are created equal.

Water soluble, chemical-based fertilizers provide plants with the macronutrients listed on the label, but because they are formed of salts, they can be harmful to healthy soil organisms. Search for organic or natural-based liquids rather than chemical salt-based fertilizers to lower the risk of fertilizer burn and provide a more balanced "meal" for your plants. A plant's health and vigor depend on a variety of trace nutrients, vitamins, amino acids, and plant hormones, all of which are present in large quantities in most natural liquid fertilizers along with the three macronutrients. You can buy a variety of liquid fertilizers at your neighborhood garden center, or in some cases, you can even make your own. The most popular kinds of natural liquid fertilizers are listed below.

By processing marine kelp at cool temperatures, liquid kelp or seaweed is produced. It is a source of various plant hormones known to help with the shoot and root growth, enhance soil structure, increase hardiness, and promote fruit development. It is also rich in many trace minerals and amino acids. According to research, liquid kelp is effective at boosting production and resisting drought. It is one of the most affordable but effective liquid fertilizers. With very little risk of fertilizer burn, liquid kelp can also be used in conjunction with any of the other items listed below.

When whole fish is cooked and filtered, fish emulsion is created. The oils and proteins are removed before the creation of the completed fertilizer emulsion for use in other products, depriving the fertilizer that results in many of the amino acids, vitamins, and hormones essential to plant growth. However, fish emulsion is an effective organic substitute for synthetic water-soluble fertilizers.

albeit an offensive one. Fish emulsion has a very potent smell, so it's best to use it only in the mornings so the smell has time to go away before dusk. If not, every cat and raccoon in the area will be content to dig up your containers in quest of dead fish.

Another, less odorous type of fish-based fertilizer is fish hydroslate (also known as liquid fish). Instead of frying the fish, hydroslate products are produced by digesting it with enzymes at a lower temperature. The partially dissolved fish is then broken up and liquefied, producing a fertilizer that is rich in nutrients and contains a variety of trace minerals.

The fish utilized in hydroslate products are either by-catch from commercial fishing or by-products from the fish farming sector.

Although some producers even add mint and other essential oils to help cover the scent, it's still a good idea to use fish hydroslates in the morning because the enzymes employed in the production process also aid in reducing the fishy stench.

These days, compost tea is gaining a lot of attention for its capacity to support healthy soil life, inhibit some illnesses, and promote optimal plant growth. But the traditional compost tea, which was made by simply letting some compost steep in the water for a few days, isn't all that it's cracked up to be. Bucket steeping's anaerobic conditions can produce some bizarre mixtures.

Compost tea today has been aerated. As a perfect mixture of high-quality compost and a microbiological food supply (typically unsulphured molasses) brews, the air is circulated through the water. A few days later, the tea is completed and prepared for use. Compost tea of the highest caliber is brimming with advantageous bacteria that are efficient at enhancing soil and plant health and thwarting foliar diseases. Although it involves several steps, making compost tea is not a challenging task. On numerous websites devoted to the subject, you can find a wealth of knowledge and how-to guides.

Compost tea brewing businesses are springing up in cities across the country, but since the tea must be consumed within a few hours of brewing, this may be a challenging business strategy.

Compost tea is a subgenre of worm tea. It is made in the same manner, with either a homebrew or industrial brewing system. However, worm castings are used to make this tea rather than conventional compost. It produces a practically odorless liquid that is full of helpful microorganisms and is ideal for watering containers and houseplants. If you have your worm bin and a reliable source of castings, worm tea is extremely beneficial.

While the goods are beneficial on their own, they are also very beneficial when mixed with other components. To make a well-rounded fertilizer and growth stimulant, natural liquid fertilizer combination products combine the goods with elements such as liquid bone meal, blood meal, feather meal, and rock phosphate.

Follow the label directions for mixing ratios and application instructions when using any natural liquid fertilizer. A hose-end fertilizer distribution system is typically used to mechanically supply the fertilizer together with the irrigation water when applying liquid fertilizers, as opposed to mixing the product in a watering can and manually watering.

When the plants in your pots are not stressed, liquid fertilizers are best absorbed. When your plants are withering or experiencing heat stress, avoid fertilizing them. For the best nutrition absorption, water them a few hours before fertilizing them.

Although using too much natural liquid fertilizer can be costly, overusing it is rare in terms of plant health. Use only what is necessary. Throughout the growing season, most liquid fertilizers should be applied every two to four weeks.

PINCHING AND DEADHEADING

Deadheading and pinching are two more recurring activities. While you can cross off these two tasks if you're producing veggies, they're necessary tasks to keep flowers and herbs in peak condition.

Deadheading

We, gardeners, refer to the process of removing the old, spent flower heads from a blossoming plant as "deadheading." By stopping the plant from setting seed, the method promotes the growth of additional flowers (and uses lots of energy to do so). The plant frequently responds to the removal of wasted flowers by producing new blooms.

Deadheading is a continuous task that starts as soon as the first peony petals fall and lasts until the last annual has been touched by frost, although the best time to do it is in the middle of the summer. Deadheading perennials like bearded iris (Iris germanica), Oriental poppies (Papaver orientale), delphiniums (Delphinium spp.), lilies (Lilium spp.), and peonies (Paeonia spp.) won't make them produce more blooms because they typically only bloom once per season. Instead, it neatens them up and helps the rest of the plant to grow more. In other words, these plants are mostly deadheaded for ornamental purposes.

However, numerous other plants bloom repeatedly throughout the growing season; these plants will continue to produce new flowers if they are routinely deadheaded.

Deadheading revitalizes the appearance of the plant as a whole and frequently produces new, fresh leaves as well. Side-buds form after the spent bloom is removed and go on to produce more flushes of flowers. Most flowering annuals and some perennials fall into this category, including garden phlox (Phlox paniculata), Shasta daisies (Leucanthemum x superbum), perennial sage (Salvia spp.), bee balm (Monarda spp.), yarrow (Achillea spp.), butterfly bushes (Buddleia spp.), coreopsis (Coreopsis spp.)

Tips for Deadheading

• For plants whose blooms grow on stalks with leaves along them, trace the faded bloom's tip back to the point where the stem's first few leaves start to emerge. Just above these leaves, snap or cut the blossom stalk. Avoid leaving a long stump behind since it can get infected with botrytis or another fungus as it rots away naturally. Butterfly bushes, Monarda, cosmos, snapdragons, black-eyed Susans, zinnias, salvias, Shasta daisies, sedums, dahlias (Dahlia spp.), and a plethora of other plants fall under this category.

• For plants like daylilies (Hemerocallis spp.), hosta, or bearded iris that have long flower stalks but no foliage along them, cut the entire flower stem all the way back to the point at the base of the plant where the foliage appears.

- Shearing back the entire plant rather than picking out the spent flowers one at a time is frequently easier for plants with mounded foliage and several little flowers. Shearing should be done once or twice during the growing season on plants like coreopsis, Bidens, sweet alyssum, French marigolds, ageratum, nepeta, dianthus (Dianthus spp.), and lavender (Lavandula spp.) to promote more blooms.
- It's not necessary to deadhead some flowering plants at all. Only a few hardy plants consistently produce new blooms and maintain a youthful appearance.

These low-maintenance plants may occasionally need to be pruned back (see the next section), but they will virtually always be in bloom. This list of plants also includes certain petunias, wax begonias, dragon- and angelwing begonias, lobelia, nemesia, torenia, oxalis, calibrachoa, and fascia (Diascia spp.).

But there is one situation in which you don't want to deadhead. Don't take away a plant's wasted blossoms if you want it to set seed on purpose. It's simple to gather and store your seed from a variety of annual, perennial, and herb flowers. Using gathered and saved seeds to launch the container garden the next year will help you save a lot of money. Easy plants to start with include cosmos, zinnias, amaranth, calendula, dill, and sunflowers.

Simply let a couple of the seed heads finish drying before cutting them from the plant and letting them finish drying for a few weeks in a cool, dry place. The seeds should then be extracted from the cracked seed heads and stored in plastic or sealed glass jars until the next spring.

To allow some of their plants to set seed for birds like goldfinches, cardinals, chickadees, and other seedeaters as late summer approaches, some gardeners also stop deadheading.

Especially if your container garden doubles as a pollinator habitat, deadheading is a crucial activity. Pollinating insects, like butterflies and bees, require a steady source of nectar, so if you want these helpful insects to remain in your yard, you must have a container garden that is perpetually in bloom. The next two projects are excellent ways to get started supporting these two important insect groups with a specially designed container garden.

CHAPTER FOUR

Troubleshooting

In a container garden, things won't always go according to plan. Vegetable plants might not yield even a single edible bite, combinations might appear more garish than anticipated, or plants might not function as effectively as you'd intended. It occurs to everyone, so don't worry. Focus on what has worked so far while continuing to develop.

This chapter's objective is to guide you through some of the challenging problems you might encounter in your container garden and give you the resources you need to quickly resolve them.

I'll start by introducing you to a few of the typical pest insects you might come across. Each pest will have a physical description, a picture, and some simple management methods. However, I've also included images and descriptions of some of the beneficial insects you might come across. These helpful insects should be promoted because they are crucial to the health of your plants. I'll then go through twelve of the most typical plant diseases and how to treat them, as well as a few physiological conditions that may be quickly fixed by altering how you take care of your containers.

Remember that starting small is one of the simplest ways for beginning gardeners to limit potential issues. In your first year, don't plant 40 containers, and don't spend a lot of money on expensive containers. Instead, concentrate on raising a few plants in repurposed containers. The beginner's project that is provided after is a fantastic way to delve into container gardening without getting overwhelmed.

GARDENING WITH MILK-CRATES
ESSENTIAL MATERIALS
cardboard milk containers
Burlap fabric roll
a mixture of potting soil and compost large enough to fill all the milk crates.

ESSENTIAL TOOLS: Scissors
Without having to spend a lot of time or money, this is yet another fantastic way to experiment with container gardening. This method is especially enjoyable because you have many design options for showing off your milk crate garden:
• To create a wall of crates, stack the planted crates in a checkerboard pattern. Use crates with taller plants, such as

peppers, eggplants, and basil, as the top tier and lower tiers for low, vining plants like cucumbers, melons, and winter squash.

- I planted the plants in the open top of the milk crate for this project, but you could also cut holes in the burlap sides and plant herbs and seeds of vining veggies right through the holes in the sides of the crate, allowing you to stack the crates on top of each other and save a ton of space.
- Milk crates make wonderful hanging planters as well. Hang the crate from ceiling hooks or plant hangers by attaching chains with S-hooks to the top edge of the container. Another excellent option to save space is to fasten the milk crates to a deck railing before planting.

When it comes to milk crate gardening, the options are unlimited!

MAKE A MILK-CRATE GARDEN: HOW TO DO IT

STEP 1: Measure the inside of the milk crate and cut a piece of natural or synthetic burlap twice that size. Use patterned or printed burlap from a fabric store for more interest. Pull the burlap ends out over the top edge of the crate and tucks them under the bottom of the crate and into the four corners. It looks much more interesting if the fabric's corners are offset from the crate's corners rather than lined up with them.

STEP 2: involves covering the burlap with the potting soil/compost mixture to a height of 1 inch above the milk crates. There is no need to make drainage holes since as you water these containers, any excess water will just drain through the porous burlap. For each carton, pick out a

single specimen plant. Do not overfill the crates because they only carry a few liters of soil each. You can add one or two filler flowers or herbs to each crate if you'd like, but don't go overboard or the plants won't grow as well.
STEP 3 Put your milk crates in whichever configuration you choose.

NOTE: Your milk crate garden may require a little more frequent watering than plants planted in non-porous plastic, metal, or glazed ceramic containers because of the burlap's porous nature.

Pest issues
Don't assume all insects are evil, leaf-eating foes. Less than 1% of the documented bug species around the world are considered pests, but the great majority are either benign or helpful. A healthy garden contains tens of thousands of species of pollinators and pest-eating beneficial insects; these creatures should be supported and unharmed.
All the control methods and products covered in this section are extremely effective and safe for the environment when used by label instructions because we don't want to harm beneficial insects while controlling the undesirable ones. They are made from naturally occurring substances that, when used properly, target the pest while causing little to no collateral damage.
But first, let me be sure to employ any physical controls as your first line of protection before applying anything to your plants. If using a product for control does become essential, always apply it according to the directions on the label, regardless of whether it is natural or organic. For

optimal outcomes and to best conserve beneficial insect species, take precautions and pay close attention to the application instructions. Even though this book isn't specifically on insects, it's impossible to discuss container gardens without mentioning insect pests. Some insects consume plants, and these herbivorous insects are only following nature's design. You will have to put up with some pest insects in your container garden.

You wouldn't have a healthy population of beneficial insects to control major pest outbreaks down the road if there weren't a few pests here and there. An overall healthy container garden is worth a few imperfect cabbage heads, some pock-marked leaves, and the rare petunia that has been slug-nibbled. We just need to develop a means to safely lower pest bug populations to a manageable level when their numbers become intolerably high and the harm, they inflict becomes excessive.

The key to effective pest control is accurate identification. If you encounter any insects in your container garden, take your time identifying them. Make use of all the tools at your disposal, and don't make assumptions about the insect before conducting careful research.

Typical Container-Garden Pests
For twenty of the pests most likely to infest your container garden, you'll find identifying details and environmentally sound management strategies below.

Aphids (many species) (many species)
All of North America's geography
Aphids are little, pear-shaped, soft-bodied insects that can

grow to be up to 1/8 in length. They can be any color—green, yellow, brown, red, gray, or even black. Some species can fly, whereas others cannot. Each aphid has two cornicles, which are tiny, tube-like structures.
Plants impacted: Nasturtiums, roses, milkweed, mums, tomatoes, lettuce, peppers, geraniums, and members of the cabbage family are among the very sensitive plants. However, there are many additional potential host plants because there are numerous types of aphids. Feeding practices and harm: Aphids consume food by penetrating plant tissue with a piercing-sucking mouthpart and sucking out the sap. They generate bent and distorted stem tips, new leaves, and buds when they feed in groups on young plant development or the undersides of leaves.
Physical controls: Aphids can be eliminated by using a hose to spray a sharp stream of water that knocks them off the plants and onto the ground, where they swiftly die. Although hand-crushing is also effective, helpful predatory insects usually naturally control aphid populations.
Horticultural oil, insecticidal soap, and pesticides based on neem are used to manage the product.

Cabbageworm (Artogeia rapae) (Artogeia rapae)
All of North America's geography
Identification: The light green caterpillars known as cabbage worms have a thin yellow stripe running down

their backs.

They are around one inch long. Adult butterflies have a 1- to 2-inch wingspan and can have up to four black dots on their wings. They are white to yellow-white in color. Caterpillars eat ragged holes in leaves, causing harm. They could also leave circular holes through broccoli and cauliflower flower clusters. Young cabbage worms might be challenging to find. Look closely for them on the midribs and undersides of leaves.

Physical restraints: To prevent the female butterflies from laying eggs on the plants, cover their favored plants with a floating row cover.

Row covers can remain in place until harvest because none of the vulnerable vegetables require pollination before being harvested. Caterpillars can be manually selected and destroyed. A lot of insectivorous birds enjoy eating cabbage worms.

Spinosad, citrus oils, botanical oils, and Bacillus thuringiensis (B. t.) are used as product controls.

All plants in the cabbage family, such as broccoli, cabbage, cauliflower, Brussels sprouts, kale, kohlrabi, radish, and turnips, are impacted.

Denver Potato Beetle (Leptinotarsa decemlineata)
All regions of North America, except for the extreme South and the Pacific Northwest. southern Canada as well
Identification: Adult beetles measuring 13 in. long have a rounded, firm shell. The head has many sporadic black patches, and the wing covers are black and tan striped. Larvae that have fully developed are 12 in. long, chubby,

reddish-pink, and have rows of black dots on their sides. All plants in the tomato family, including tobacco, potatoes, eggplants, and tomatoes, are affected.
Feeding habits and destruction: Larvae and adults of the Colorado potato beetle quickly skeletonize leaves. The topmost leaves of the plant are where you'll typically find them. Pellets of their black waste could also be discovered.

Physical controls: Place a floating row cover over the potato plants and keep it in place until harvest. Handpick the adults and larvae from tomatoes and other crops every few days. Rotate crops and remove garden waste to prevent adult beetles from overwintering.

Bacillus thuringiensis (B. t.) var. San Diego or B. t var. tenebrionid, spinosad- and neem-based insecticides are effective product controls.

cucumber bug (striped species: Acalymma vittata; spotted species: Diabrotica undecimpunctata Howard)
All of North America's geography
Identification: Striped and spotted common species mature to a length of 14 inches. Striped beetles are bright yellow as adults and have three distinct black stripes. Spotted cucumber beetles have eleven (eastern species) or twelve (western species) black spots on their wing coverings and are greenish-yellow in color. Larvae eat plant roots when they are underground.
All plants in the cucurbit family, such as cucumbers, melons, pumpkins, and squash, are affected. Beans, corn, beets, potatoes, tomatoes, asparagus, flowers, and soft

fruits are some other plants that may occasionally be harmed.

Feeding practices and damage: Feeding harms leaves and blossoms with a few small, ragged holes. The potential of cucumber beetles to spread the deadly bacterial wilt to plants, however, is their major drawback.

Plant only cucumber types that are bacterial wilt resistant as physical controls. When susceptible plants are young, cover them with a floating row cover; when the plant flower, remove the floating row cover. To catch the adult beetles, place yellow sticky cards above the plant tops. As soon as they are planted, mulch young seedlings with loose material, such as straw or hay, to prevent female insects from getting to the soil to lay their eggs.

Neem, spinosad, and pyrethrins are the product controls.

Beetle Flea (many species)
All of North America's geography
Identification: These flea-like beetle relatives are incredibly tiny, measuring barely 1/10 of an inch long. Although some species are iridescent or striped, the majority are shiny and black. They are frequently spotted jumping about damaged plants and moving quite swiftly. The flea beetle can harm a wide range of plants, but some of its preferred targets are cole crops, maize, eggplant, pepper, potatoes, radishes, tomatoes, and turnips.

Feeding habits and damage: Flea bugs leave behind extremely recognizable damage. little, round
The plant has holes that give the appearance that it has been shot with tiny buckshot. The larvae can cause minor

harm to potato tubers and plant roots because they live underground.

Physical controls: To draw and capture adult beetles, place yellow sticky cards directly above the plant tops. While floating row cover is ineffective at keeping flea beetles away from plants in an in-ground vegetable garden (it frequently results in trapping the beetles as they emerge from their underground pupation), it is effective at keeping the insects away from containerized plants, particularly if they were planted in a fresh batch of potting mix at the beginning of the season.

Citrus oil, garlic oil, kaolin clay-based sprays, hot pepper wax, neem, and spinosad are among the products that are controlled.

Plant bug with four lines (Poecilocapsus lineatus)
The geographical range of North America: south of Canada and east of the Rockies
Four-lined plant bugs can be recognized by their swift movement. They feature four black lines running the length of their greenish-yellow wing coverings. At maturity, adults are one-fourth of an inch long, but they begin life as tiny, red, and black nymphs in the early spring.

Plants impacted: Plants with intensely scented foliage are what these insects are most drawn to. Their favorite foods include basil, lavender, mint, oregano, and sage, but you can also find them eating ornamental plants like azaleas, Russian sage, peonies, mums, Shasta daisies, and viburnums, among many others.

Damage caused by the four-lined plant-insect is obvious.

Feeding habits. On the young plant leaf, there are clusters of small, sunken, spherical pockmarks. The insect's piercing and sucking mouthpart are what causes the harm. The pockmarks eventually become brown, and the injured tissue may come loose and leave tiny holes in the leaves. They only inflict cosmetic harm, which is easily repairable.

Physical restraints: These insects only produce one generation annually, in the early summer, and they live for four to six weeks. After feeding damage has stopped, remove the affected plant material in the middle to end of the summer. Until midsummer, when the insects are no longer active, protect susceptible plants with floating row cover.

Product controls: Since most of the damage caused by products is cosmetic, they rarely need to be implemented.

Mushroom Gnats (Bradysia species and Lycoriella species)
Geographical range in North America: all; regarded as an indoor annoyance pest

Identification: Mature gnats are small, black, 1/8-inch-long flies that have a lifespan of around two weeks. Females lay their eggs in soil fissures at this time. The resulting translucent, tiny larvae can also eat fine roots and plant debris, but they mostly eat the various fungi growing in potting soil. They pupate into adults in the soil within a few weeks, and the cycle continues with multiple generations existing concurrently at any given time. A strong indication that anything is wrong occurs when a cloud of small, black flies erupts from the pot of a houseplant. If there are hundreds of mature fungus gnats in that cloud, they are difficult to overlook even though they are individually undetectable.

Plants at risk include all houseplants.

Feeding habits and plant damage: Because fungus gnat larvae primarily eat fungi found in potting soil, these insects rarely seriously harm infected plants. The plant may, however, wilt and exhibit signs of stunted growth in extreme situations where the larvae also feed on the plant roots.

Physical controls: Constantly wet soils encourage the growth of fungi, which is a great source of food for larvae. Most fungus gnat problems can be resolved by simply watering less. Only water-contaminated houseplants when the soil is completely dry and infrequently. Make sure both the saucer bottom and the pot itself have excellent drainage.

Unable to hold any standing water. Repot the plant in fresh, sterile potting soil if this doesn't solve the issue. On yellow or blue sticky cards positioned vertically an inch or two above the soil surface, you can also catch adult fungus gnats. Another option is to completely remove the top half-inch of potting soil and replace it with something that resembles small gravel, like Gnat Nix or chicken grit.

Product regulations: Beneficial nematodes (Steinernema feltiae) and Bti (Bacillus thuringiensis var. israelensis) can be sprayed or drenched into the soil as powerful biological control agents. The first is a tiny nematode that eats the gnat larvae by tunneling into the earth. The second is a biological insecticide that kills gnat larvae by using a particular strain of bacteria. One well-known brand is Gnatrol®.

Asian Beetle (Popillia japonica)

Geographical range in North America: Populations are concentrated primarily east of the Mississippi River and north into the lower portion of Canada, but they are present in most of the country, except the extreme Southeast.

Identification: Adult beetles are 12 inches long and 14 inches wide, and they are metallic green with copper wing covers. When threatened, they raise their two hind legs, and when startled, they drop plants. The plump, grayish-white, C-shaped larvae that live on the ground have light brown heads.

Affected plants: Adults consume more than 300 different landscaping plants. Favorites include zinnias, roses, rhubarb, blueberries, raspberries, and grapes, among many others. Grubs consume turf grass and a variety of ornamental plants' roots as food underground.

Adults skeletonize leaves and harm floral buds in their feeding habits. They appear in the summertime and eat most heavily when the temperature is between 85° and 95°F. Grub damage appears as uneven brown patches that peel back like carpets in the lawn.

Physical controls: Let your lawn go dormant throughout the summer months while females are depositing eggs. The population for the following year is decreased because the eggs require moisture to survive. Adult beetles should be thrown into a jar of soapy water. Early and frequent handpicking of the adults reduces the number of congregating pheromones that the beetles release to attract additional beetles for mating. If possible, keep

Japanese beetle traps away from your container garden. These traps appear to draw more beetles than they catch, according to several studies.

Product controls: When given to the lawn every spring, beneficial nematodes (Heterorhabditis species or Steinernema carporcapsae) are extraordinarily efficient against the grubs. Neem and spinosad are effective product controls to combat adult Japanese beetles.

Leafhoppers (many species) (many species)
All of North America's geography
Identification: Adults are thin, wedge-shaped insects that can grow up to 1/4 in. long. They might be brilliantly colored, green, yellow, or brown. When startled, leafhoppers will scoot sideways like a crab or jump. Nymphs resemble adults, although they are smaller and lack wings. On the undersides of leaves, adults and nymphs of the leafhopper are frequently seen together. On the undersides of leaves, leafhoppers' old, molted skins and dark feces flecks can occasionally be seen.

Plants impacted: Leafhoppers feed on hundreds of different species, many of which have unique host requirements. Roses, potatoes, grapes, beans, lettuce, beets, and a variety of other plants make excellent hosts.

Feeding habits and damage: The insect's sap-sucking behavior results in mottled stippling or pale patches on infected leaves, which are signs of feeding damage. The plant's leaves may curl up and fall off if they are severely injured. Some leafhopper species spread different plant diseases, causing issues beyond just the damage they cause by feeding on plants.

Physical controls: Leafhoppers are a little challenging to manage because of their quick movement.

In unbowed regions and crop detritus, adults spend the winter. To reduce overwintering sites, clear the debris as soon as the last garden harvest is completed. Early in the season, use floating row covers to protect plants against leafhopper damage.

Product controls: Horticultural oil and insecticidal soap both help to lower populations, but it's crucial to cover the undersides of the leaves while spraying. Pyrethrins also have some effectiveness.

Green Miner (many species)

All of North America's geography

Identification: Although you rarely see the insects themselves, leaf miner damage is very simple to notice in your landscape. The larvae of several distinct fly species are known as leaf miners. Approximately 14 in long, adult flies frequently have black bodies with yellow patterns. Small, green, or brown maggots that eat inside plant leaves are the larvae.

Plants impacted: Various leaf-mining species feed on

various plant types. Spinach, Swiss chard, beets, hollies, columbine, nasturtiums, peas, blueberries, and boxwood are a few examples of some of the most likely victims. Damage caused by these tunneling insects' feeding habits is the "mining" out of the tissue in between the layers of leaf tissue. They leave behind squiggly trails and blotches on the leaves as undeniable signs of their presence. Most of the time, their harm isn't bad enough to call for utilizing any kind of control solutions. Most of the damage is cosmetic, especially to decorative plants.

Physical controls: The adult leaf miners cannot lay eggs on the leaves of spinach, beet, or chard plants if a layer of floating row cover is placed over the plants. If you do notice their recognizable squiggly eating pattern on a leaf, just clip it off and throw it away. Beets and chard should not be planted until after the lilacs bloom since then the kind of leaf miner that they host is dormant. In addition, several parasitic wasp species that deposit their eggs within leaf miners while they are still inside the leaf aid in the eradication of these pests. By putting herbs like dill, fennel, and cilantro in your container garden, you may promote these beneficial insects. The tiny parasite wasps that do not sting eat the nectar from these three plants.

Product controls: Neem and spinosad are the most efficient spray treatments for managing leaf miner maggots because they are tucked away between layers of plant tissue. Hot pepper wax sprayed early in the season prevents females from laying eggs on any plants.

Mealybugs (many species) (several species)

All of North America's geography

Mealybugs are 1/8 in. long, oval-shaped, and typically covered in a soft white or gray fluff for identification. Smaller larval mealybugs and adult females both pierce and suck sap from plants with their mouthparts. They frequently create clumps of wax or fuzz after feeding in groups. Males only survive long enough to reproduce and do not eat. These insects produce honeydew, a sticky excretion. It leaves both the infected plant itself and anything below it with a shiny, tacky residue.

Plants that may be affected include citrus, grapes, fruit trees, orchids, hibiscus, dracaena, focus, and many other common hosts.

Feeding habits and damage: Plants that are severely infested may experience stunted or deformed growth. Mealybugs in small quantities won't do much harm, but in high numbers, defoliation may result. Although they are widespread pests of indoor plants and greenhouses, these insects are more prevalent outdoors in warm, humid regions of North America.

Physical controls: Mealybugs can be easily eradicated from plants by rubbing cotton balls or squares soaked in isopropyl rubbing alcohol on the stems and leaf surfaces. Insects are also driven off plants by a strong stream of water. Houseplants shouldn't be overfed because mealybugs love overfed plants.

Product inhibitors: Neem, horticultural oil, citrus oil, pyrethrins, insecticidal soap.

Spanish Bean Beetle (Epilachna varivestis)

Geographical range in North America: from southern Canada east of the Rockies in the United States. Additionally prevalent in a few Western US locations.
Identification: Adult beetles have a huge ladybug-like appearance. They have wing pads that are copper in color with sixteen black spots on them. 13 long, pale yellow larvae have delicate, bristly spines covering them.
All beans, including green beans, pole beans, runner beans, snap beans, lima beans, and soybeans, are possible hosts for the disease.
Feeding preferences and plant damage: Mexican bean beetles occasionally eat developing beans and blossoms in addition to skeletonizing leaves, leaving only the veins unharmed. Most frequently, larvae are discovered on the undersides of leaves.
Physical controls: When you find larvae or adults, take them up by hand and crush them. Despite having spines, the larvae are flexible and squishy. To reduce the population of Mexican bean beetles, a tiny, non-stinging predatory wasp from India called Pediobius foveolatus is regularly distributed in several Eastern states. When Mexican bean beetle larvae are present, you can buy the larval wasps to release in your garden.
Spinosad, hot pepper wax and citrus oil are used as product controls.

Scales (many species) (many species)
All of North America's geography
Identification: Both soft and hard scales are present. Both have pierced, armor-like mouthparts for feeding and can develop strong shells. Some species appear as tiny, white flecks, while others resemble raised bumps on twigs, leaves, and leaf petioles. Some species may also have a downy fuzz covering, and most of them emit sticky honeydew, which is visible on infected plants as a shiny, sticky film.
Plants impacted: The majority of scale species feed on a particular plant species or set of plant species. Magnolia, Pachysandra, fruit trees, dogwood, lilac, birch, euonymus, holly, citrus, boxwood, and many others are examples of common hosts.
Damage and feeding patterns: Severe scale infestations may result in stunted growth and yellow foliage. Additionally, stems and branches may become weaker. Because both wasps and ants feed on the sticky honeydew secreted by some species of scale, both insects are frequently seen on plants with scale infestations.
Physical controls: You can physically crush large species of scale by tracing your fingertips along the length of a branch that is infested with them, smashing the insects as you go. Avoid overfeeding since scale reproduces more quickly on overfertilized plants. A cotton ball or square dipped in isopropyl rubbing alcohol can be used to wipe away certain scales.
Control of the product can be challenging due to the

strong, armor-like shell that many species of scale have. Several weeks out of every year, certain species go through a soft, crawling stage of life, which is the ideal period to attempt and manage them. However, because the crawler stage of each species of scale develops at a different time, more research is necessary. Neem, horticultural oil, and insecticidal soap are examples of useful items.

Slugs/Snails (various species) (several species)
All of North America's geography
Snails and slugs are land mollusks that come in a variety of colors, including gray, black, orange, brown, tan, and yellow. Slugs lack outer shells, whereas snails do. Both expel a slimy coating that they use to both protect themselves and glide. The first indication of their presence is frequently their distinctive slime trails. Snails and slugs both feed primarily at night, but they also emerge on cloudy or wet days.
Many flowering plants and vegetables, including lettuce, tomatoes, strawberries, hosta, and many others, as well as nearly all young seedlings are vulnerable.
Both slugs and snails have a mouth coated with small teeth that shred plant material in a manner much to a cheese grater.
They leave uneven holes in the middle or edge of leaves. Examine plants at night because this offender is frequently absent throughout the day.
Physical controls: Encourage birds, snakes, salamanders, frogs, toads, turtles, and ground beetles because many

different animals eat slugs. To prevent evening feeding on damp vegetation, only water in the morning. Copper strips around vulnerable plants give slugs a minor jolt (the slime reacts to contact with copper).

Any that you locate, handpick them and drop them into a cup of soapy water. Beer saucers also work well for catching slugs, but they need to be cleaned out every day. The use of baits containing metaldehyde or methiocarb is prohibited. Pets and other creatures are severely poisoned by these products. Instead, surround plants with iron phosphate-based baits.

Banana Bugs (Anasa tristis)
All of North America's geography
Adult squash bugs are about 5/8 in. in length and are dark brown or grayish in appearance. Their bodies are oval-shaped and flattened. Young nymphs have spindly legs, no wings, and black patterns. They frequently gather in groups to eat.

When squash bugs are crushed, an awful smell comes out in all stages. Bronze-colored eggs are placed in clusters on the undersides of leaves.

All cucurbit crops, such as cucumbers, melons, pumpkins, squash, and zucchini, are affected.

Squash bugs feed by puncturing the plant with their mouthpart that resembles a needle and sucking out the sap. They leave behind specks that quickly turn yellow and could cause the death of leaves. Vines that are severely infested wilt and become crispy. Squash bugs frequently congregate in large numbers on the ground near infested plants and around fruit stems.

Start by planting resistant types as a physical barrier. Keep vulnerable plants off the ground by using trellises and protect young plants with floating row cover until they begin to bloom. Handpick the adults and nymphs frequently and crush any egg clusters you come across. Product controls: Pyrethrins and neem are both effective against nymphs.

Pumpkin Vine Borer (Melitta satyriniformis)
Geographical range in North America: From the southeast of Canada up into all of the United States east of the Rocky Mountains.
Identification: Adult moths have clear wings and are red and black. They are active during the day.
They are 112 inches long and resemble huge hornets more than moths. The vine borers are the larvae. Before pupating into an adult, these plump white caterpillars, which have brown heads, can reach lengths of up to an inch. Eggs are typically placed at the base of the plant, just above or below soil level, and are flat and brown in color. All members of the cucumber family, including winter and summer squash, pumpkins, gourds, melons, and occasionally cucumbers, are potential host plants.
Feeding habits and damage: Rapid plant wilting is a sign of

borer damage. At the base of the plant, frass (the borer's excrement) is frequently seen, and occasionally a hole too. In the spring, adults emerge from their underground pupation. Soon after, eggs are laid, and the larvae spend just over a month eating the plant stem's inner tissue. Usually, there are two generations per year.

Physical controls: After planting, cover vulnerable crops with a floating row cover and keep it in place until the plant's flowers enable pollination. Slice up the afflicted stems with a razor blade if you spot the borer damage before the plant dies, then dig out and kill the pest inside. Add soil over the cut area. As soon as the plant sprouts its first true leaves, you can also wrap a 1 x 6 in. strip of aluminum foil around the base of the plant. Place the strip's bottom edge just below the soil's surface. This protects the plant's most delicate area and prevents female vine borer moths from laying their eggs there.

Product controls are challenging because the borer is located inside the facility itself. However, you can immediately inject Bacillus thuringiensis (B.t.) into any borer holes at the base of the stem, and it will kill any insects within. Insecticidal soap can also be sprayed around the base of the vine once a week to smother any eggs laid there.

Mite spiders (several species)
All of North America's geography
Identification: To observe this small spider and tick relatives, you'll need a microscope. Spider mites are only 120 in length and have eight legs. Large colonies of them

spin delicate webbing for shelter as a group. Most gardeners first see the webbing before they see the mites. Shake the plant over a sheet of white paper and look for tiny particles moving around for certain identification.

Plants impacted: The two-spotted spider mite, the most prevalent species, feeds on more than 180 distinct plant types. Azalea, miniature Alberta spruce, grapes, melons, phlox, and strawberries are just a few examples of host plants.

Damage from spider mites is manifested as mottled, yellow foliage. The stems and undersides of leaves frequently have thin webbing on them. Mites can readily migrate over the landscape since the wind can carry them from plant to plant.

Physical controls: Spider mite populations are drastically reduced by beneficial predatory insects like big-eyed bugs, damsel bugs, ladybugs, predatory mites, and tiny pirate bugs. Encourage them by filling your container garden with numerous blossoming herbs and other little blooms.

Product controls: A few chemical insecticides promote the development of mites. Avoid spraying whenever possible because these treatments also harm the beneficial insects that naturally regulate mite populations. Horticultural oil and insecticidal soap are good product controls, if necessary.

Geranium and tobacco budworms (Heliothis virescens)
The geographical range in North America includes the

eastern and southeastern United States as well as southern Canada. They might also exist in several western states. Tobacco/geranium budworm adults are nocturnal moths, according to the identification. They have three dark brown bands across the wings and are light brown in color. Plants are not harmed by the adults, but the larvae eat plant foliage and flower buds. Depending on their life stage and source of food, caterpillars range in color from yellow to green to brown to pink or maroon, measuring up to an inch in length.

Plants impacted: Nicotiana (flowering tobacco), zinnias, petunias, geraniums, ageratum, marigolds, snapdragons, verbena, portulaca, and other flowers' flower buds are frequently eaten by tobacco/geranium budworms.

Additionally, they might consume some vegetable harvests including tomatoes, collards, and okra.

Feeding habits and damage: Tobacco/geranium budworms are normally unable to withstand harsh winters, but as the climate changes, they are moving further north. The first signs of damage are holes in flower petals or missing or unopened flower buds. Budworms can swiftly eat away at a plant's flower buds, leaving the plant with ragged, damaged flowers. They will also devour leaves if there aren't any flower buds accessible. Budworms can be seen all year round in the south but are more common late in the season in the north.

Budworm caterpillars are most active in the evening. Go outside and handpick anything you find in the garden. Bacillus thuringiensis (B.t.) products are excellent for product controls. Spinosad is an additional choice.

Hornworms of tobacco and tomatoes (Manduca quinquemaculata and Manduca sexta)

All of North America's geography

Hornworms, sometimes known as sphinx or hawk moth larvae, are the enormous, green larvae of nocturnal moths. A mature caterpillar can reach a length of 5 inches. Pupae develop underground.

Members of the nightshade family of plants, such as tomatoes, tobacco, potatoes, peppers, and eggplants, are impacted.

Gardeners frequently discover the dark pellets of hornworm excrement left behind before they notice the caterpillars themselves. On plant tops where the caterpillars feed at night, damage in the form of missing leaves is initially noticed. During the day, they hide under or on inside leaves, making them frequently difficult to locate.

Physical controls: Non-stinging parasitic wasps that employ hornworms as hosts for their growing offspring frequently feast on them. Under the caterpillar's skin, the cotesia wasp lays eggs that will eventually hatch into larval wasps. The hornworm's interior is consumed by the larval wasps, who quickly break through its skin to create exterior cocoons. Avoid disturbing hornworms that have white, rice-like sacks hanging from their backs since they have already finished feeding and will soon perish. Hornworms can also be picked up by hand from plants. Product controls such as Bacillus thuringiensis (B.t.) and spinosad are effective but rarely required. When you're growing a small number of plants, handpicking is far more productive.

Whiteflies (Trialeurodes vaporariorum and several additional species) (Trialeurodes vaporariorum and several other species)
Geographical range in North America: all. North has a year-round greenhouse and indoor pests. In the northern summer, outdoor pests. In the southern regions, active all year long.
Identification: Adult whiteflies measure just 120 to 110 in. and are tiny, white, moth-like flies. When disturbed, infested plants release a cloud of flying insects. They produce honeydew, a delicious excretion that coats adjacent plants and other surfaces with a glistening, sticky coating. Whitefly larvae are quite small and lack wings. Whiteflies can live on almost any plant, but frequent hosts include poinsettias, blooming tobacco, tomatoes, geraniums, sweet potatoes, citrus trees, and bedding plants.

Damage: Both adult and young whiteflies feed by suckling plant juices from the undersides of leaves. Except in the south, outdoor populations rarely cause major harm. Whiteflies can be a major concern in greenhouses where populations can increase significantly. Whitefly eating weakens plants, induces wilt and leaf drop, and yellows foliage.
Physical controls: Yellow adhesive cards put just above plant tops are a simple way to trap whiteflies.
Neem, citrus oil, hot pepper wax, horticultural oil, and

insecticidal soap are some of the product controls.

The bulk of the beneficial insects you'll see in your container garden is not detrimental to your plants. Some aid you by eating troublesome insects, while others fertilize crops or decompose organic materials. The seven typical parasitic, predatory, and pest-eating insects listed below can be seen scavenging about your plants in quest of their next meal. All can be found in a variety of North American garden habitats.

A syrphid or Hover Flies
Many species of hoverflies have an abdomen that is striped in black and yellow, giving them the appearance of little wasps or bees, however, they are harmless to people and do not sting. The 14 to 12-in.-long adults, which are crucial pollinators, may hover while consuming flower nectar. Pests are managed by larvae. Small, brown, or green maggots called hoverfly larvae to hatch from eggs put on pest-infested plants.
Up to 500 bugs can be consumed by each larva before it matures. Adults require pollen to procreate, and as they lack specialized mouthparts (unlike many other beneficial insects), they are drawn to plants with shallow blooms. Excellent selections for your container plantings are alyssum, aster, coreopsis, cosmos, daisies, fennel, mint, sunflowers, wild mustard, and dill. Make sure your container garden has something blooming from the last spring frost to the first fall frost to maintain a steady population of these predators.

Lacewings in green

These lovely, delicate insects are drawn to lights and are frequently seen clinging to window screens at night in the summer. The adults have large, transparent wings, threadlike antennae, and golden eyes. They are pale green in color. They have a length of up to an inch and only eat pollen and nectar. The eggs of adult green lacewings are laid on the tips of long filaments, and when arranged in a row along a blade of grass, they resemble tiny lollipops. These eggs develop into flattened, swiftly moving, brown, and white lacewing larvae, which have huge, curved mandibles for catching prey.

Even though they are barely a half-inch long, they may eat up to 100 aphids every day, earning them the name "aphid lions." Angelica, caraway, coreopsis, goldenrod, yarrow, and tansy should all be present in your container garden to entice them.

Ladybird, Lady Beetle, or Ladybug

Ladybugs, which have over 480 different species in North America, are probably the most well-known of all the helpful insects. But not every ladybug has a red body and black spots on it. Depending on the species, ladybugs can be yellow, cream, brown, orange, black, gray, or pink in color. There may be many spots on them or none. They can have black bands going down their wing covers, or they can be stripped, mottled, or both. However, ladybugs are beneficial for the garden regardless of their coloration. These insects are between 1/6 and 1/2 inches long, but all of them have six hard wing covers and are dome-shaped.

Upscale scale, mites, mealybugs, tiny caterpillars, whiteflies, mites, and psyllids are just a few examples of the common pests that ladybugs eat. Nearly all ladybugs are predators. It's equally crucial to remember that ladybug larvae also consume nuisance insects. Ladybug larvae could appear a little frightening because they resemble miniature, flattened, six-legged alligators, but they are quite beneficial for the garden. Planting their preferred nectar sources in your container garden can naturally promote a healthy population of these critical insects because adult ladybugs need to consume a protector to breed. Caraway, cilantro, dill, fennel, sunflowers, cosmlace flowers, and lace flower are all beneficial plants.

One thing to keep in mind is that you shouldn't buy ladybugs from your neighborhood nursery and release them into your garden. The majority of ladybugs you'll discover for sale belongs to a species known as the convergent ladybug, which is wild-collected in several regions of the American West during its huge winter hibernation. After that, they are packaged and distributed for sale across the nation. This is a risky practice because it not only has an impact on the wild populations of this ladybug but also has the potential to infect other wild ladybug populations with diseases. Only buy ladybugs raised in insectaria if you plan to release them.

Small Pirate Bugs

These little creatures are the smallest of the predatory true bugs that are frequently discovered in North American backyards. The oval-shaped adult, which is only 1/8 in.

long, is black with white wing patches. The nymphs in the form of a teardrop are considerably smaller and either orange or yellow in hue. Both animals move surprisingly quickly and feed by piercing their victim with a mouthpart that resembles a needle. Spider mites, thrips, aphids, insect eggs, tiny caterpillars, lace bugs, scale, whiteflies, and other pests are among the things these minute pirate bugs eat. Plant a bunch of spring-flowering plants in your container garden to draw them in. Minuscule pirate bugs rely on early-season pollen and plant sap as a food source because they are frequently the first predators to appear in the spring before prey becomes easily accessible. Plants like a basket of gold, oregano, sage, wallflower, sweet alyssum, red clover, and parsley are good selections for this useful insect.

Wasps with parasites
In North America, parasitic wasp species number approximately 6,000 different varieties. One of the most helpful insects in the garden, these little non-stinging wasps are reported to parasitize over 300 different pest species. The majority of parasitic wasp species range in length from 1/32 to 1/2 inches. Even though some species have pointed ovipositors that resemble enlarged stingers, these are only utilized to deposit eggs. Eggs are often laid within or on host insects by female wasps. When the eggs hatch, the prey is eventually killed by being consumed. Some species, like the cotesia wasp that hunts tomato hornworms, pupate in exterior cocoons, while others pupate inside their hosts' bodies (like the tiny Aphidius wasp that attacks aphid colonies). Aphids, beetle larvae,

bagworms, cabbage worms, potato beetles, maize earworms, cucumber beetles, cutworms, caterpillars, Japanese beetles, leafminers, sawfly larvae, squash vine borers, and many more pests can all be controlled by wasps, depending on the species. Allium, alyssum, cosmos, dill, fennel, thyme, yarrow, coneflowers, sunflowers, helianthus, and other plants attract adult wasps, which eat nectar and pollen.

Spiders
Spiders are arachnids, not insects, yet they nevertheless have a lot to offer gardeners. In the world, there are 38,000 different species of spiders. While some species have hair, some don't. They come in a variety of hues, from dull brown to dazzling white, vibrant yellow, or other combinations of vivid colors. They liquefy an insect and "drink" it to catch their prey and obtain food. Depending on its size and area of expertise, each spider has a different diet of insects to consume, yet all spiders are predators. Aphids, asparagus beetles, Colorado potato beetles, cutworms, various pest caterpillars, lace bugs, spider mites, squash bugs, and many other pests can all be eliminated from your garden with their assistance. Spiders can live in any sheltered spot and find it to be a safe habitat.

Fly Tachinids
With 1,300 different species, this is the biggest and most significant group of parasitic flies in North America. Adults have little, bristly wings that resemble miniature houseflies. They range in length from 1/3 to 3/4 inches.

While their young are the pest eaters, adult flies are crucial pollinators. Because female tachinid flies directly lay eggs or leave larvae on the bodies of host insects like different caterpillars, beetles, squash bugs, sawfly larvae, four-lined plant bugs, and many more, they are parasitoids. The host is consumed and eventually killed as the larvae tunnel into its body after the eggs hatch. Some species will also lay their eggs on plants in the hopes that a host will eat the plant, which will then absorb the eggs. The fly larva typically pupates inside its host before emerging as an adult.

Tachinid adult flies are drawn to gardens and containers with a lot of flowering herbs, especially those in the dill (Apiaceae) family since they feed on nectar and pollen. They like plants from the daisy family, such as aster, chamomile, feverfew, ox-eye daisy, coreopsis, and Shasta daisies, as well as cilantro, dill, fennel, golden Alexander, and parsley.

By interplanting vegetables with flowering annuals and herbs, you can give these beneficial insects access to nectar and pollen, which is one of the best ways to ensure that there are plenty of "good" bugs in your container garden. The plants used in the upcoming initiative are some of the most effective at luring and sustaining beneficial, pest-eating insects.

CHAPTER FIVE

Seasonal and Harvesting Considerations

It might be challenging to picture how a container garden will look after the growing season when it is first planted at the beginning of the growing season. Every growing season can be surprising, even after experience teaches you what to anticipate.

Most gardeners experience a blend of awe and exhilaration with a dash of disappointment to keep us in our place. Most of the time, you find yourself exclaiming, "I can't believe I grew that!" You might, however, occasionally express regret by saying, "I can't believe I killed that." All of it relates to gardening.

Even though nature is unpredictable in general, many parts of it are not. Birth and death are cyclical processes that occur repeatedly throughout nature. Predictable aspects of nature include the changing of the seasons, animal migration patterns, plant dormancy, and the life cycle of butterflies. Of course, the two major ones are the seasons changing and the life cycles of the plants we grow—cycles we can anticipate and take advantage of. It could be as easy as planting a pepper in the spring so that you get fruits in the summer before the plant is killed by frost, or it could be as complex as including a late-blooming perennial to provide nectar for migrating monarchs. Gardeners always consider the cyclical, predictable aspects of nature while making decisions.

As we take care of our gardens during the growing season, we also consider the natural cycles. While frost-sensitive basil is planted in the late spring, after the threat of freezing weather has gone, flowering bulbs like daffodils and tulips are planted in the fall so they have time to develop roots before blossoming the following spring. We plant crops that prefer chilly temperatures very early or very late in the growing season, such as lettuce and radish, and we pick garlic when the plants start to die back in the height of summer. Gardeners carry out a variety of tasks in a predictable way, taking advantage of several cues from nature to time everything as precisely as we can. This chapter moves on from Chapters 1 and 2, which guided you through the first stage of container gardening, and Chapters 3 and 4, which focused on cultural approaches and problem-solving. In the first section of this chapter, we advance through the growing season cycle once more and concentrate on the moment when your plants are ready to be harvested. You'll pick up useful advice on how to maximize the harvest, the time it just right, and lengthen the shelf life of your homegrown produce. This chapter's second section explores what transpires as fall approaches and the year completes its cycle. I'll provide some fantastic suggestions for repurposing end-of-season containers as holiday decorations.

There are also instructions on how to properly empty and store your containers throughout the winter to maximize their life as well as instructions on how to overwinter plants.

HARVESTING

Contrary to popular belief, harvesting happens intermittently during most of the growing season in container gardens that are home to a variety of vegetables. The types of fruits and vegetables you are cultivating will determine when you will harvest them. In essence, you'll be harvesting as required. Here are some suggestions to help you get the most out of some of the more popular crops you could be producing in your container vegetable garden, both in terms of yields and shelf life.

Pay close attention to the "days to maturity" listed on each variety's seed packet or nursery pot tag. This figure represents the length of time needed for a certain plant to mature. For many crops, there is a lot of variation in the days to maturity. For instance, while most sweet potato varieties take about 110 days to reach harvest readiness, radishes, one of the fastest-growing vegetable crops, mature in as little as 30 to 45 days. Consider this crucial number when designing your garden and make your plans accordingly.

Many different crops have higher yields when they are continually harvested. For vegetables like tomatoes, eggplants, peppers, cucumbers, beans, peas, and the like, whose edible portion is a fruit or legume that develops from a flower, the more often you harvest the ripe vegetables, the more flowers the plant produces, extending the harvest and production of the plant. In other words, most of these plant varieties produce more vegetables the more you pick them.

Root vegetables like carrots, turnips, beets, and radishes can be dug up from the ground and consumed at any stage of development rather than becoming "ripe" in the traditional sense. They can either be harvested as "baby vegetables" when they are still young or they can wait until they are fully mature before being picked. Everything depends on the flavor and texture you want to achieve. Unwashed root vegetables can be kept in the refrigerator in a bag or a root cellar or cold basement in a box. For the longest shelf life, root vegetables can also be buried in a container of damp sand. Keep the container filled with sand in a basement or root cellar that gets cold but doesn't freeze. One of the simplest root vegetables to cultivate in containers is beets. The following project demonstrates a cool method for cultivating a lovely mixture of beets and Swiss chard in a distinctive elevated planter.

ROBERT K. BRANTON

CHAPTER SIX

Additional Container Concepts

Growing in containers offers practically infinite options, and while there's no doubt that your imagination serves as the best muse, a little extra inspiration never hurts. There's nothing wrong with taking a little inspiration from another gardener whose style you like or can easily adjust to meet your own. Sometimes the best container designs are an extension of a brilliant concept someone else had first. You may get your creative juices flowing in a variety of settings, including garden tours, public gardens, publications, blogs, and books like this one.

Ten additional container gardening ideas that can be readily adapted to many various gardening styles will be covered in this chapter. If the plants are the proper size physically for the container, all these concepts are scalable and easily adaptable to whatever plants you'd like to cultivate.

PLANTERS FOR TABLES

Having a live centerpiece can make it simple to green up your outdoor living space. Decorate side tables, beverage carts, bistro tables, outdoor bars, and other small surfaces on your patio, deck, or balcony with pint-sized tabletop plants. On a larger dining table or outdoor couch table, put three or four small tabletop plants together. For a larger outdoor dining table, a single large pot filled with edible or flowering plants works wonders as a centerpiece. For good design, choose an oblong container for an oval or rectangular table and a round container for a table that is circular.

Additional inventive suggestions for tabletop pots:

- If you're hosting a dinner party, you might want to make a small individual planter to put on each guest's seat. After the celebration, send each guest home with a planter and a potted plant bearing their name or a motivational message.
- Tiny tree seedlings or bonsai in containers make attractive tabletop additions. These tiny trees are always a

focal point, even though they need routine care and careful pruning to keep their size.

- Culinary herbs in containers are the ideal plant selection for live centerpieces since they can be cut to size and added to salads and sandwiches as they are served.
- Use a bundt cake pan that has a few drainage holes added to plant your centerpiece on patio tables with umbrellas. Succulents, herbs, annual flowering plants, or other interesting plants can be placed inside the pan by inserting the umbrella through the hole in the center of the pan.

POTS OF STRAWBERRY

Tall planters called "strawberry pots" have external holes or pockets that are spaced irregularly. Because they aid promote air circulation, keep the ripening fruit off the ground, and let you grow numerous berry plants in a relatively small space, they are typically used for producing strawberries. But strawberry pots also have some drawbacks, including the fact that they can be challenging to plant, some kinds dry up rapidly, and the plants frequently grow unevenly. However, these flaws can be easily fixed with a few little adjustments. Strawberry pots are great containers for growing a variety of plants, especially when space is limited, such as vegetables, greens, herbs, and flowers.

- Porous clay strawberry pots dry out extremely rapidly. Instead, choose one made of plastic or glazed ceramic, or seal the terracotta before planting by applying two layers of sealer. Instead of flat holes, seek out strawberry pots with deep pockets. The pockets provide more space for root expansion and are better at collecting irrigation water.

- Water frequently flows out the side holes when strawberry pots are watered from the top rather than soaking into the soil. One way to prevent this is to plant a piece of PVC pipe through the middle of the pot that has 1/2-inch holes drilled through it. The irrigation water is put into the hollow pipe, where the holes allow it to slowly permeate the surrounding soil.

- Don't try to force plants into your strawberry pot through the holes after filling it with soil. As an alternative, fill the pot to the rim of the lowest holes, then plant from the inside out by forcing the plant's top through the hole. Instead of forcing a large root ball inside the hole from the outside, it is much simpler to gently jimmy the foliage out of the hole. Once the plants are in position, continue to fill the pot with potting mix until you reach the bottom of the next series of holes, and then repeat the process to the top.

- If you can rotate your strawberry pot a quarter turn every few days to make sure all the plants get enough sunlight. This will help prevent uneven growth.

MINIATURES AND FAIRY GARDENS

Children take great satisfaction in helping to create and maintain fairy gardens, which are a very whimsical addition to any container garden. Small plants are combined with tiny decorations like dollhouse-sized furniture, fairy houses, and other tiny adornments in fairy gardens. Designing a container of miniatures for these make-believe garden creatures is a lot of fun, and small garden visitors will enjoy using it.

Here are a few simple ways to create your own containerized fairy garden, even though fairy gardening is a distinct art form with several books devoted to it and an entire plant collection chosen, bred, and sold for it.

- Fairy gardens can be created using wheelbarrows that have a few extra drainage holes. Wheelbarrows are portable and sit at the ideal height for enquiring little hands and eyes. The wheelbarrow should be filled with planting mix, several dwarf or small plants should be chosen, arranged, and planted there, and finally, a fairy house, some stepping stones, and other accents should be added.

- To create a themed fairy garden, decide on your favorite fairy tale, narrative, or film and design the garden around that idea. Make a tiny gingerbread home out of small terracotta tiles and white caulk if Hansel and Gretel is a favorite story. Or, for those who adore mermaids, create a fairy garden with an underwater theme by covering the ground with sand, glass pebbles, and smooth sea glass and adding succulents with tiny, oblong leaves that resemble bubbles. Finish it off with a little boat raised on a stack of rocks, a few inches above the sand.

- Fairy gardens can be sweet and simple or quite ornate. A toddler will notice even a little pot by the back entrance. Do not feel that you must go above and beyond to please the young gardener in your life. The secret is to give them as much freedom as possible to touch, feel, and arrange the accents in your fairy garden.

HANGING AND VERTICAL PLANTERS

Growing up or down instead of out is a terrific way to use vertical gardens and hanging planters. They add additional growing areas to practically any site, conserve space, and cover disused, vacant walls. In addition, a well-placed, free-standing vertical planter can improve aesthetics while also enhancing privacy, lowering noise levels, and providing shade for dining spaces.

There are numerous approaches to vertical growth, each having advantages and disadvantages. Items like wood pallets, plastic water bottles, picture frames, rain gutters, used buckets, hanging shoe organizers, plastic or metal pipes, and scrap lumber, to mention a few, can easily be salvaged or reused into vertical planters.

Numerous commercially available vertical planting systems are also available, such as fabric pouches to hang on walls, fences, or other vertical structures, free-standing planter "walls," and wheeled, mobile gardens with multiple tiers.

Another efficient technique to make extra room for your plants to flourish is hanging planters. Growing food or ornamentals, filling empty vertical space, or adding a pop of color to an otherwise boring space are all possible with hanging baskets and other types of hanging wall planters.

WATER GARDENS IN CONTAINER

A small-scale habitat for birds, frogs, dragonflies, and other aquatic species, containerized water gardens that house a small fountain or bubbler is simple to build and maintain. They also provide the sound of moving water to the landscape. Even a few fish can be added to your patio water garden; they will consume the mosquito larvae and provide another interesting aspect.

Water gardens in containers can be straightforward or intricate, big, or small. A container, a few plants, and water are all that is required. Building a bamboo fountain to recirculate the water in the pot is part of the upcoming project, which goes beyond simply building a patio water garden.

You have several options for preserving your water garden over the winter when the growing season is over. The first step is to empty the pot and bring the plants indoors for the winter. For the winter, most water plants can be kept in a tub of water in a cool basement or garage where they will go into dormancy. The water garden might even spend the entire winter outside. Hardy aquatic plant species can be kept within the pot over the winter, but a birdbath warmer is required to prevent the water

from freezing solid. Stick with plastic, acrylic, or other frost-proof container materials if you intend to leave your container outside during the winter for a longer lifespan.

Until spring arrives, turn off the fountain and relocate the pump indoors.

Container water gardens are simple to maintain.

You don't ever need to change the water in your container; simply top it out as needed during the season with rainwater you've gathered or dechlorinated tap water. If mosquitoes do become an issue, float a circular mosquito cake composed of the biological insecticide Bti (Bacillus thuringiensis var. israelensis), often known as a "mosquito dip," in the container. Mosquitoes rarely become a problem if the water is being circulated. Fish, plants, or other aquatic life won't be harmed by it.

HOW BALCONY GARDENING SAVED MY MARRIAGE

Made in United States
Troutdale, OR
07/07/2023